Overcoming Compassion Fatigue offers an invaluable resource that will benefit all practitioners – rookies and veterans alike. This well-researched workbook is filled with practical self-assessment tools and concrete strategies for detection, intervention and prevention. Integrating CBT techniques provides a unique and very hands-on approach to managing compassion fatigue and related symptoms of caregiver stress. *Overcoming Compassion Fatigue* is a much needed addition to our field and I look forward to sharing it with my colleagues and students.

Françoise Mathieu, M.Ed., CCC, author of *The Compassion Fatigue Workbook: Creative Tools for Transforming Compassion Fatigue and Vicarious Traumatization*

This is an excellent book that addresses an important and timely topic for anyone working in the helping profession. It is well written and engaging, and provides assessment measures and helpful exercises that are invaluable to the reader. I highly recommend to anyone who is a care provider.

Frank M. Dattilio, Ph.D., ABPP, Department of Psychiatry, Harvard Medical School

Martha Teater and John Ludgate offer a generous gift to practitioners in the caring professions with their book *Overcoming Compassion Fatigue: A Practical Resilience Workbook*. They nudge the reader with many self-awareness inventories and checklists to be mindful of the message---remember to practice self-care as you offer others care. The writing is clear, compelling and instructive. This is a gem of a contribution to the self-care and resiliency literature!

Tom Skovholt, Ph.D., LP author of *The Resilient Practitioner and Becoming a Therapist*

This is a must read for all levels of psychotherapists in the human service and mental health fields. This CBT Model, self help guide offers information on burnout, risks, and rewards of the helping profession. This workbook is a great resource to take care of ourselves to remain active and happy. I highly recommend this easy-to-read book and plan on sharing it with my staff.

Rudy Flora, LCSW, ACSW, CSOTP co-author of *How to Work With Sex Offenders (2nd Edition)*

OVERCOMING COMPASSION FATIGUE

A Practical Resilience Workbook

By

Martha Teater, MA, LMFT, LPC, LCAS

John Ludgate, PhD

PESI
Publishing
& Media
www.pesipublishing.com

Copyright © 2014 by Martha Teater and John Ludgate

Published by
PESI Publishing & Media
PESI, Inc
3839 White Ave
Eau Claire, WI 54703

Cover Design: Amy Rubenzer
Layout Design: Bookmasters
Edited by: Marietta Whittlesey

Printed in the United States of America

ISBN: 978-1-937661-44-1

PESI
Publishing
& Media
www.pesipublishing.com

For Don, with gratitude and much love.

And for our family:
Luke, Betsey, and Nora
Kevin and Heather

And with thanks to all those who have entrusted me with their stories through the years.
—Martha

For the three best antidotes to my stress, my sons Daniel, Matthew and Conor.
And with appreciation to the many clients over more than three decades who have taught me so much.
—John

Acknowledgements

It is with a deep sense of gratitude that we acknowledge the contributions of so many who expanded our knowledge of both compassion fatigue and cognitive behavioral therapy.

First and foremost, we thank the pioneers who led the way in compassion fatigue identification, treatment, and prevention: Francoise Mathieu, Dr. Charles Figley, Dr. Beth Hudnall-Stamm, Dr. Laurie Anne Pearlman, Dr. John Norcross, Dr. Thomas Skovholt, and others.

Our understanding of CBT would be limited were it not for leaders in the field such as Dr. Aaron Beck, who changed the course of psychotherapy and the fate of innumerable clients indirectly through his writing, research and teaching, and also inspirational mentors such as Dr. Ivy Blackburn, Dr. Fred Wright, Dr. Robert Berchick and Dr. David M. Clark.

What we know about compassion fatigue and CBT might have remained abstract and detached if it weren't for the many people who have shared their stories with us. Heartfelt thanks go to our clients, our professional peers and thousands of workshop participants who have openly given us glimpses into their lives. We owe a debt to so many, and it is our hope that this workbook might be a small repayment of all that we've been given.

This workbook has been sharpened by the keen eye and skilled touch of Linda Jackson at PESI Publishing and Media. Linda patiently and expertly guided this whole process, helping us develop a workbook that is focused and clear. Thanks also to our editor, Marietta Whittlesey, who organized our material into a more well-defined whole. We are both appreciative of the good people at PESI/CMI Education for enabling us to hit the road as professional trainers, giving us the rich experience of getting to know thousands of clinicians and hone our skills as professionals.

Finally, we thank the many clinicians who honor us by courageously sharing their stories. It's a privilege to work in this field, and it's not one we take lightly.

Thank you.
Martha Teater
John Ludgate

Martha's Preface

Like many of you, I started my career with enthusiasm and idealism. I had high hopes and the lofty expectation that I could have an impact on people and really make a difference for individuals and families.

I have always been an empathetic person, curious about people and relationships. Even as a teenager I sought depth in friendships and thrived while delving into why people did what they did. . . what made people tick. A college degree in social work led me to my first job as a nursing home social worker, an experience that was a surprisingly rich learning experience. After getting a master's in counseling, I became licensed as a marriage and family therapist, professional counselor and clinical addictions specialist. I worked in addictions, integrated healthcare and indigent medical care, and have had a private practice since 1990.

So how does my enthusiasm and idealism compare to what it was way back when? I'm probably not the only one of us who has seen it wax and wane through the years. When a client does well. . . my energy is high. Someone relapses, continues to struggle, or doesn't seem to get better. . . let's just say that my optimism sags.

My interest in compassion fatigue came as a direct result of Hurricane Katrina. As a Red Cross volunteer, I spent my first disaster mental health deployment in a shelter in the Gulf Coast. During that time I met many local mental health workers who were suffering similar losses to the people they were helping. I returned home to my usual work routine, but couldn't get those helpers off my mind. How would they cope with the despair all around them while so many were going through traumas and losses of their own?

I've also seen plenty of people go through trauma and struggles during other disaster mental health deployments following floods, fires, tornadoes and other devastating events.

These experiences have clearly shown me how important it is to take care of ourselves so we can better help others. Whether or not you think of yourself as a trauma worker, if you work with people on an intimate level, you are exposed to their pain and deep emotions.

My training in cognitive behavioral therapy opened my eyes to some powerful interventions we can use to keep ourselves whole and well in spite of the challenges of our work. CBT pioneer, John Ludgate, has a wealth of experience in this area, and I was honored when he suggested we collaborate on this workbook. His keen insights and vast knowledge have inspired me, and I'm sure will help our readers as well. John and I aren't immune to the difficulties that helpers face. We are both practicing therapists dealing with hurting people. We both use the tools that we share in this workbook and can attest to their usefulness.

I'm convinced that the only way to enjoy this work for the long haul is to take care of yourself *first*. When you fly on an airplane you'll hear the reminder from the flight attendant to put the oxygen mask on yourself before helping others. If we don't keep ourselves well and strong we become useless as helpers. Our hope in writing this workbook is to offer concrete, practical tools for you to use to keep yourself energized to do the work you are called to do. By using these strategies you will be able to not only survive, but thrive as a helping professional.

John's Preface

I have been a practicing cognitive behavior therapist for several decades. Over my years of training I have learned a lot about specific disorders and interventions but have learned more by experience how to deal with the inherent stresses of being a caregiver dealing with humans in pain and distress. There were a number of formative experiences over my career which got me interested in this topic of caregiver distress and eventually lead to the book *Heal Yourself: A CBT Approach to Reducing Therapist Distress and Increasing Therapeutic Effectiveness* (2012) and more recently to collaborating with Martha Teater on this workbook.

While engaged in post-doctoral training some years ago, I was pleased to see that a training workshop on the topic of therapist emotional reactions, and how to manage them, had been scheduled for my training class. However, I also realized that this was the first time in over eight years of training in clinical psychology that such a workshop had been offered to me. My fellow trainees had had the same experience. Over many years subsequently of surveying supervisees and trainees, I have found that both initial graduate courses and postgraduate training programs continue to pay little or no attention to this issue of care providers dealing with their own emotions, thoughts and behaviors, triggered by client or clinical situations. So essentially we are left to fend for ourselves.

I can recall how shocked I was several years ago when I heard that a very prominent cognitive behavior therapist, who I knew slightly, and who ironically wrote articles about the need for self-care, had committed suicide. He had many colleagues and friends all over the world. So I couldn't help but wonder: did he ever talk about his issues with anyone? Did anyone notice his distress? We will never know but it raises the question, how can we better look after ourselves and others in this demanding field we work in? Two years ago I learned with great concern about the death by suicide of two cognitive behavior therapists in Ireland, my country of origin. It led me (and their CBT colleagues) to wonder how we can be more attentive to distress signals in our peers and how we can intervene skillfully and sensitively, if necessary.

When I needed some short-term therapeutic help at an earlier stage in my life, I know I had trouble in initiating this process. Why? An analysis of my own anxiety and shame reactions uncovered some dysfunctional beliefs such as: "I should be in control of my emotions, since I know all this stuff," a belief I would have challenged actively in any of my clients. I would guess that dysfunctional beliefs about seeking help or admitting there are problems probably exist for many health care providers.

I also realized at an early point in my career, when reflecting on my belief systems and how they interacted with stressors in my job, that I derived a great deal of my self-worth from my performance as a therapist—which of course I judged rather narrowly by the progress clients made in therapy with me. As a consequence, I took negative outcomes and clients' relapses very personally and suffered a good deal of personal stress. This pattern of dysfunctional thinking, I quickly realized, is a recipe for distress and since then I have actively monitored and challenged this form of thinking in myself. Likewise, in my capacity as a supervisor, I have over the years tried to focus on the therapists' emotional and cognitive responses as much as the clients' problems to ensure that supervisees do not fall into such traps.

Being conscious of how important a topic this is, in part due to some of the above experiences, and knowing how little there is in the literature or in current training courses to guide providers through their own stress reactions, I decided to approach Martha Teater, my fellow author, whose stellar work in the area of compassion fatigue I was familiar with. To my delight, she allowed herself to be talked into this project and has been an invaluable collaborator.

I love my work and find it very rewarding. I am sometimes amazed that I get paid to do what is so inherently satisfying and inspiring. I am also all too human, and so am distressed at times by what I encounter. Our aim in this workbook is to share with you, our readers, some practical strategies to make this journey, which all of us are on, more enriching and less taxing.

Author Bios

Martha Teater, MA, LMFT, LPC, LCAS, has a wealth of experience as an international compassion fatigue educator and consultant. She has trained thousands of healthcare and mental health clinicians in detecting, intervening, and preventing compassion fatigue. A seasoned professional, Martha earned a bachelor's degree in social work from Miami University in Oxford, Ohio, and a master's degree in counseling from Ohio State University. She is a licensed marriage and family therapist, a licensed professional counselor, and a licensed clinical addictions specialist. Martha has maintained a private practice in marriage and family therapy in Waynesville, North Carolina, since 1990. Martha is a trained cognitive behavioral therapist and is a Diplomate with the Academy of Cognitive Therapy. As an American Red Cross disaster mental health volunteer, Martha has been deployed many times to provide support to traumatized people across the country. She is a co-leader of national and international Red Cross support programs.

Martha is a prolific writer, having published over 175 articles in newspapers and magazines including *Family Therapy Magazine* and *Psychotherapy Networker*.

John Ludgate, PhD, is a licensed psychologist who has worked as a psychotherapist for almost 30 years. He currently works at the CBT Center of Western North Carolina, located in Asheville, North Carolina. He specializes in treating mood, anxiety, relationship and psychosexual disorders. As well as having an active clinical practice, he is involved in training and supervision in CBT. He obtained a bachelor's degree in psychology from Trinity College, Dublin, a master's degree in clinical psychology from University of Edinburgh in Scotland and a PhD from Trinity College.

He trained at the Center for Cognitive Therapy under Dr. Aaron Beck, the founder of Cognitive Therapy, obtaining a Postdoctoral Fellowship in Cognitive Therapy from the University of Pennsylvania. He subsequently became Assistant Director of Training at Dr. Beck's Center. In the early 1990's Dr. Ludgate was a Research Clinical Psychologist at the University of Oxford in England and served as a cognitive behavioral therapist in several outcome studies of panic disorder, agoraphobia, social phobia and hypochondriasis. He subsequently worked as a clinical psychologist in state agencies and private practice.

He has published the book *Maximizing Psychotherapeutic Gains and Preventing Relapse in Emotionally Distressed Clients* and was co-editor with Beck and others of *Cognitive Therapy with Inpatients: Developing a Cognitive Milieu*. He published *Cognitive behavioral Therapy and Relapse Prevention for Depression and Anxiety* and *Heal Yourself: A CBT Approach to Reducing Therapist Distress and Increasing Therapeutic Effectiveness*. He has written numerous journal articles and book chapters in the field of cognitive behavior therapy for anxiety and depression. He has presented many seminars and workshops on cognitive behavioral approaches, both nationally and internationally. He is a Founding Fellow of the Academy of Cognitive Therapy, serves on the Credentialing Committee of the Academy and is a member of the Association for Behavioral and Cognitive Therapy (ABCT).

Table of Contents

Chapter 5: Intervention **69**

Chapter 6: Prevention **113**

Chapter 1
Overview

INTRODUCTION

Working as a helping professional can bring deep satisfaction and lasting rewards. But the ability to help people through working as a nurse, social worker, counselor, teacher, psychologist, health care provider or other helping professional may also have a negative impact on the practitioner. This book aims to help you better grasp the potential downside of this work and equip you with practical tools to help you manage your work differently and minimize your risk of harm from doing this work. You will find that this book is not academic, detached or highbrow. We write this as fellow travelers along this journey, using the same tools we share with you to help ourselves as we carry on in this privileged task of helping others. Our purpose is to share effective ways for you to prevent caregiver stress and, if you already have symptoms, to help you manage them and find effective ways to rise above your current challenges and find renewal in your work.

In some ways we can liken this to a long car journey. Your starting point is where you are here and now. The destination is fulfillment in both your career and your personal life. The goal is to make this journey safely and successfully and not break down on the way, be involved in an accident or take wrong turns adding to the time and stress in travelling. To maximize our chances of reaching our destination safely and having a successful trip, several things need to happen.

- During the journey we need to be aware of and recognize any issues which could arise and jeopardize our progress. This is covered in the **Detection** section. Inside the car we would need to be aware of early warning signs (fuel and temperature indicators, engine noises that are abnormal), which is equivalent to recognizing our own personal early warning signs of stress.

- Conditions outside the car (other drivers' behavior, road and weather conditions) will also need to be taken into account to be safe while driving. These are high risk situations (client or organizational stressors) which can cause us to become burned out or overly stressed.

- If we should experience some problems on the journey (wrong turn, mechanical failure, fender bender) we need to get the car back on the road. This is discussed in the **Intervention** section, which will be helpful to us when under stress professionally.

- Some interventions, as will be described later, can be self-directed (we can consult the map and get back on the right road, fix the flat tire ourselves), some will involve getting others help (fellow drivers, pedestrians, state police) and others will involve more professional help (tow truck, AAA).

- We must prepare for the journey well (have the car in good working condition, check oil, gas, and tire pressure). We should make sure we have the right tools in case of a flat tire or other needs along the way. We need to make sure the driver is not tired starting out or otherwise compromised in some way. We'll cover these issues in the **Prevention** section.

- We should develop an emergency plan, which should be thought through beforehand.

Let's get started. It's time to hit the road.

OVERVIEW: THE RISKS OF YOUR JOURNEY

Any journey comes with risk. Just getting on the road means that certain things can happen. You could get a flat tire, an engine part could go bad or you could have a car accident.

Good planning can lower your risk somewhat, but it's not possible to anticipate or prevent every unfortunate occurrence.

Working as a helping professional puts you at risk; just as driving a car opens you up to certain potential consequences.

Let's look at the risks inherent in your journey of helping others.

THE COSTS AND CONSEQUENCES OF CARING

"The expectation that we can be immersed in suffering and loss daily and not be touched by it is as unrealistic as expecting to be able to walk through water without getting wet."
—R.N. Remen

There are several names for it: compassion fatigue, caregiver stress, secondary traumatization, vicarious traumatization, compassion stress, caregiver fatigue, bystander effect and trauma exposure response, among others. Some might insert the term burnout here. But burnout, while sharing some signs and symptoms with these conditions, is different as we shall see further on.

Caregiver Stress

Whatever you choose to call it, caregiver stress or compassion fatigue is a very real and expected consequence of working with people who have experienced or are experiencing trauma and suffering. Helpers can absorb the suffering of others and end up feeling weary and worn from this secondary traumatic exposure. We don't need to have experienced the trauma first-hand. The trauma exposure leading to caregiver stress is indirect, but it can lead to profound emotional and physical consequences. You may be experiencing some symptoms yourself. If so, it's our hope that by reading this book and completing the exercises within, you'll find relief from your current challenges, and you can prevent further impact down the road.

BURNOUT CHARACTERISTICS

"Burnout is a depletion or exhaustion of a person's mental and physical resources attributed to his or her prolonged yet unsuccessful striving toward unrealistic expectations, internally or externally derived."
—H. Freudenberger

"Oh, you hate your job? Why didn't you say so? There's a support group for that.
It is called EVERYBODY, and they meet at the bar."
—Drew Carey

Top 10 signs you are suffering from burnout

1. *You're so tired you now answer the phone "Hell."*
2. *Your friends call to ask how you've been, and you immediately scream, "Get off my back!"*
3. *Your garbage can is your inbox.*
4. *You wake up because your bed is on fire, but go back to sleep because you just don't care.*
5. *You have so much on your mind you've forgotten how to pee.*
6. *Visions of the upcoming weekend help you make it through Monday.*
7. *You sleep more at work than at home.*
8. *You leave for a party and instinctively bring your briefcase.*
9. *Your phone exploded a week ago.*
10. *You think about how relaxing it would be if you were in jail right now.*

                                                                    —Anonymous

As we noted earlier, people often think that what they are experiencing is burnout when in fact they are experiencing caregiver stress or vice versa. The main difference between burnout and compassion fatigue is exposure to trauma and suffering. Anyone in any job can experience burnout. People who work in any role in restaurants, stores, businesses and institutions can experience burnout. This is generally unrelated to trauma exposure.

As opposed to caregiver stress, which as we have seen, can be a result of absorbing the suffering of others, burnout is usually related to administrative, organizational or political issues at work. This term was first introduced by Maslach (1982) to describe a collection of symptoms including emotional exhaustion, depersonalization and reduced personal accomplishment.

The Maslach Burnout Inventory (Maslach, Jackson & Leiter, 1996) describes three aspects of burnout:

1. Emotional exhaustion ("I feel emotionally drained by my work")
2. Depersonalization ("I worry that my job is hardening me emotionally")
3. Reduced personal accomplishment ("I don't feel that I'm positively influencing other people's lives through my work")

The Burnout Measure (BM) developed by Pines and Aronson (1978) measures the following:

1. Physical exhaustion (feeling tired or rundown)
2. Emotional exhaustion (feeling depressed or hopeless)
3. Mental exhaustion (feeling disillusioned or resentful)

With burnout you may feel little control over your work environment and decision-making. Often it feels like there is a brutal combination of a high workload and few rewards. There may be a lot of stress in the work environment and a feeling of being unsupported by administration. Inadequate training and supervision contributes to this. Values or ethical conflicts may intensify burnout. The risk of burnout increases when caregivers feel moral distress at work and must do things with which they disagree or are morally opposed.

Other factors contributing to burnout include:

- Burdensome agency policies
- Documentation demands
- More work than time to do it
- High expectations by management
- External locus of control
- Tight deadlines
- Unrealistic vision of what can be done
- Little autonomy and independence

> It is possible to have both burnout and caregiver stress at the same time, which is a challenging combination.

Helping professionals may experience burnout due to administrative issues at work, and they may have compassion fatigue or caregiver stress because of the exposure to the intense emotional material of those with whom they work. It is possible to have both burnout and compassion fatigue at the same time, which is a challenging combination. Nevertheless, the tools for fixing them are essentially the same.

TRANSIENT WORK-RELATED STRESS RESPONSE

Both compassion fatigue and burnout, if unrecognized and unaddressed, can be serious, pervasive and likely to be incapacitating over a period of time. At a somewhat milder and less impairing level, health care workers may experience distress that may be more situational or transient and possibly related to encountering specific stressors (client-related or organizational) during a particular time frame (days or weeks). The stress response or distress triggered may be significant emotionally, behaviorally and cognitively but typically endures for briefer periods of time or episodically.

For example, 36% of psychologists say they frequently experience stress in their work (Clay, 2011), while 85% of emergency room nurses indicated that they had experienced some symptoms related to stress in the previous week (Wicks, 2006). While these transient symptoms and effects are not as severe as those associated with compassion fatigue and burnout they are still problematic for those who experience them.

The following brief checklist may be used as a quick screening for work-related distress and could indicate that some issues related to the onset and maintenance of this level of stress may need to be addressed. The key is the onset and duration of your symptoms. For example, if you normally sleep well and have a good sense of humor and now you can't fall asleep and rarely find anything funny anymore, you may be experiencing transient work-related stress.

You may **temporarily:**

- Feel anxious or apprehensive
- Get tired easily and frequently
- Argue with others over minor things or have low frustration tolerance
- Be unable to relax
- Feel beset by demands or under pressure
- Experience lack of patience or tolerance towards clients and others
- Feel there is not enough time for yourself, family or friends
- Experience some memory and concentration lapses
- Lack interest in or time to socialize or engage in recreational activities

- Feel irritable
- Experience sleep or appetite disturbances
- Develop a critical or cynical attitude toward work or life
- Get little satisfaction from usually enjoyable activities
- Feel unfulfilled at the end of the workday

Readers will note that the symptoms of compassion fatigue and burnout include many of the above but typically to a much greater degree, for longer periods of time and with more significant associated impairment. Nevertheless, the strategies for more effective self-care, which will be described later, apply equally to those who experience transient distress but who would not meet conventional criteria for either of the more severe conditions. All caregivers, both professional and familial, are at risk for this challenging set of concerns. Studies have shown that these symptoms are present in all helping disciplines, including:

Counselors	Substance abuse professionals
Social workers	Health care professionals
Nurses	Humanitarian workers
Doctors	Children's and adult protective services workers
Veterinarians	
Psychologists	Journalists
Teachers	Clergy and chaplains
First responders	Hospice workers
Law enforcement officers	Funeral home staff
Animal control officers	Hospital employees
Firefighters	

RISKS AND REWARDS OF HELPING

> We are not referring to the most difficult story you have ever heard, we are talking about the thousands of stories you don't even remember hearing.

Taking a road trip has risks inherent to it. There are a lot of unforeseen events that could take place and mess up our trip, cost money or be inconvenient. Yet most of us get in vehicles every day, deciding that the risk is worth the reward.

We have to be realistic about the risks inherent in our work as helpers, because being aware of possible dangers to ourselves will help us identify and prevent them in ourselves and in those around us such as professional colleagues, supervisees, students or interns. Knowing this, we continue to work as helping professionals, because we have weighed the costs and benefits. We usually decide the benefit is worth the risk! The risks may be quite subtle. Compassion fatigue and burnout take time to set in. As noted compassion fatigue educator Francoise Mathieu (2011) stated: "*We are not referring to the most difficult story you have ever heard, we are talking about the thousands of stories you don't even remember hearing.*"

In general, risks come from client behavior and issues, work conditions and professional isolation. The list below refers to hazards for psychotherapists, but it's relevant for virtually all helping professionals and even for caretakers of elderly or ill family members.

Client Issues

- Client behaviors that cause problems may include suicidality, chronic depression, extreme anxiety, resistance, dependency, anger and volatility, lack of involvement toward positive change, non-compliance and transference issues.
- Client medical issues, such as chronic or terminal illness and chronic pain may complicate the work and also lead to both provider and client stress.

Working conditions

Hazards can also come from the work setting itself. Working conditions that contribute to caregiver stress and burnout risks include:

- Office politics, documentation demands, heavy caseloads and lack of administrative support all contribute. Working in an autocratic agency with high demands on staff, but a low priority placed on staff satisfaction or fulfillment, can lead to burnout and compassion fatigue. This is particularly true if the therapist has received little or no training in coping with the stressful emotional reactions triggered by working in the health care field. Professional isolation can become an issue partly due to the constraints of confidentiality, agency structure, limited peer support and poor self-care.

Personal Risk Factors

- Emotional depletion can be caused by taking your work home with you, determining your own value by the outcome of your clients and the ongoing drain of hearing stories of sadness and struggle. This is magnified if you have a great deal of non-work stress in your personal life.
- The risk of emotional depletion can be modified by provider psychological characteristics such as emotional resiliency and coping or problem solving skills.

Let's balance this heavy list of risks by looking at some of the very real and rich rewards that can come from a career as a helping professional.

Rewards of this work

"There is richness to the experience of relating on an intimate level with many people."
—P.P. Heppner

Norcross and Guy (2007) found that psychologists are consistently satisfied in their work. He noted that in his 44 years of research, psychologists' job satisfaction was never lower than 88%. In contrast, job satisfaction was around 80-81% among physicians providing direct client care. In a study comparing the rewards of performing psychotherapy versus those of engaging in psychological research, Radeke and Mahoney (2000) found some significant differences. For example, 94% of the psychotherapists, but only 78% of the researchers, agreed that their work "made me a better person." Agreement was better (92% and 81%, respectively) that the work "made me a wiser person." Ninety-two percent of psychotherapists stated that their work increased their self-awareness compared with 69% of researchers.

Other rewards of this kind of work that are frequently cited in surveys of care givers include intellectual stimulation, the satisfaction of helping others and an increased capacity to enjoy life.

Some care providers even state that the work feels like a form of spiritual service. In addition:

- Most helpers express pleasure at being able to reduce distress in the people they serve.
- Many feel honored to be connected with others on an intimate level. They realize it's a gift to be trusted to engage with others in a very deep and meaningful way.
- There is an intellectual and emotional challenge to being "in the moment" with people and trying to figure out what will be helpful in "real time."
- The work can be challenging and spontaneous. It's important to intervene in ways that will be helpful and not cause harm.
- Working with people provides unlimited variety and stimulation. No two people are the same. This work is rarely boring.

> Many of us feel that we are doing what we were born to do, that our work is a natural extension of ourselves.

When considering the risks and rewards of being in a helping profession, it's important to recognize that some of the very same aspects of the work that can be the most rewarding can also *most increase our risk*. Unlike many other occupations, where work can easily be left at the door, helping is often a part of the identity of the helper. Many of us feel that we are doing what we were born to do, that our work is a natural extension of ourselves.

Signs and symptoms of caregiver stress

Even as you are reaping enormous rewards from your work, you may at the same time be suffering from some degree of caregiver stress or burnout without even knowing it. Many different symptoms can indicate that a problem has developed or is likely to arise in the future. Caregiver stress and burnout can affect a person in many different ways:

Psychological

Being easily frustrated	Anger at perpetrator or causal event
Irritability	Guilt
Annoyance	Loss of a sense of personal safety and control
Isolation	
Sadness	Feeling more vulnerable to danger
Feeling inadequate or ineffective	Depersonalizing others
Negativity	Sense of humor becomes darker, more cynical or sarcastic
Intrusive thoughts or images related to someone's suffering	Negative self-image
Preoccupation	Depressive symptoms
Difficulty feeling tender, warm, intimate emotions	Reduced empathy
	Resentment
Detachment	Less pleasure in work

Physical

Headaches	Elevated blood sugar
Stomach complaints	Fatigue and exhaustion
Muscle tension	Sleep problems
Increased blood pressure	Increased susceptibility to illness

Behavioral

Hyper alert	Difficulty thinking clearly
Restless	Trouble making decisions
Jumpy	Greater use of alcohol or other drugs
Nervous	Reduced sex drive
Easily startled	Anger
Hypervigilance	Exaggerated sense of responsibility
Change in response to violence: numb or increased sensitivity	Forgetfulness
	Difficulty with personal relationships

At work

Feeling overwhelmed by client needs	Work life and personal life bleed into each other
Decreased commitment to work	Less compassion toward those you serve
Resentment toward employer	Over-functioning
Increased tardiness or absences	Seeing yourself as being indispensable
Poor boundaries	

Cognitive

Many people with caregiver stress or burnout notice some cognitive shifts that become problematic. McCann and Pearlman (1990) report that this can be seen in the areas of:

Dependency/trust (suspicion of others)

Safety (feeling more vulnerable to danger)

Power (feeling helpless)

Independence (loss of control and freedom)

Esteem (being bitter or cynical about others)

Intimacy (alienation)

Frame of reference (blaming the victim)

Some of us feel guilty when the burden of caring is weighing on us. Herman (1997) reports that many helpers feel guilty for having *not* been traumatized in the way that the person we're helping has been. We also may feel guilty for the suffering that a person feels *due to* our intervention. Herman (1997) notes that we should remind ourselves that we are working toward healing and wholeness with trauma survivors; we aren't just retraumatizing them without a purpose. Courtois (2009) cautions that we need to balance our view of others as either victims or survivors. If we see everyone as victims we trivialize their experiences. If we see people solely as survivors we may not acknowledge the price they paid for the suffering they've experienced.

SIGNS AND SYMPTOMS OF COMPASSION FATIGUE AND BURNOUT

The symptoms of caregiver stress and burnout can impact us in many important areas of life. Carefully consider these signs of stress and note how they impact you personally. You may find it helpful to note on the worksheet below how these symptoms are expressed in your life.

Psychological signs

I am easily frustrated, irritable or annoyed.

_____

_____

I tend to isolate myself and avoid people.

_____

_____

There are times that I feel more sadness than the situation calls for.

_____

_____

Sometimes I feel inadequate or ineffective.

_____

_____

My attitude has become more negative.

_____

_____

I have intrusive thoughts or images of someone else's suffering or trauma.

_____

_____

I have become preoccupied with the suffering of others.

_____

_____

There are times that I have difficulty feeling tender, warm, intimate emotions.

_____

_____

I have felt detached or different from other people.

_____

_____

I have felt anger at the perpetrator or causal event of someone's pain.

_____

_____

I have experienced vague feelings of guilt.

_____

_____

There are times when I feel a loss of personal safety and control and more vulnerability to danger.

_____

_____

Sometimes it appears that my work has hardened me to other people.

_____

_____

There's been a change in my sense of humor; it's become darker and more cynical or sarcastic.

_____

_____

I see myself in a more negative light.

_____

_____

I've had some signs of depression (sadness, loss of interest in things I used to enjoy, social isolation, etc...).

_____

_____

I'm less sensitive and empathetic than I used to be.

_____

_____

I've been more resentful and angry.

_____

_____

I'm enjoying my work less.

_____

_____

Physical signs

I've had more physical concerns (headaches, stomach upset, more illnesses, high blood pressure, etc. . .).

_____

_____

I get more sore and achy than I used to.

_____

_____

My sleep habits have changed or I'm fatigued.

_____

_____

My health isn't as good as it used to be.

_____

_____

Behavioral signs

I'm over-alert, restless, jumpy, nervous or easily startled.

_____

_____

I'm more hypervigilant or aware of my surroundings.

_____

_____

I see a change in my response to violence: I'm numb or more sensitive to it.

_____

_____

I've had difficulty thinking clearly or trouble making decisions.

_____

_____

I'm using alcohol or other drugs more than usual.

_____

_____

There is a change in my desire for intimacy or my desire for sex is lower.

_____

_____

I'm acting angrier and have a shorter fuse.

_____

_____

I have an exaggerated sense of responsibility and feel too many things fall to me to do.

_____

_____

I'm more forgetful.

_____

_____

I've had difficulty with personal relationships and am not as easy to get along with as I used to be.

_____

_____

Signs at work

I feel overwhelmed by the needs of others around me.

_____

_____

I'm less committed to my work.

_____

_____

I've had some resentment toward my employer.

_____

_____

I've missed work at times, or I've shown up late.

_____

_____

My boundaries are different, either too rigid or too loose.

_____

_____

My work life and personal life aren't very well separated.

_____

_____

I'm becoming less compassionate and empathetic.

_____

_____

YOU'RE NOT THE ONLY ONE FEELING THIS WAY

You are not alone! It's estimated that 13% of the working population suffers from burnout (Bahrer-Kohler, 2013). The prevalence of caregiver stress and/or burnout is high among helping professionals. Some 79% of hospice nurses have moderate to high rates of compassion fatigue (Wicks, 2006). Half of child welfare workers are severely impacted, as are 54% of medical residents (Borritz, Rugulies, Bjorner, Villadsen, Mikelson & Krisitensen, 2006). American surgeons indicate that they think about suicide 1.5-3 times more than the general population; only 26% of those who thought about suicide sought help (Beyond Blue, 2013).

> There is an interaction between certain client or work stressors and the personality of the helper, with both contributing to the risks they may encounter.

Mental health specialists have been found to be at high risk for burnout (Onyett, Pilinger & Muijen, 1997). A 2011 survey by American Psychological Association showed that 36% of psychologists said they felt stressed out during their work day and 20% described high levels of stress (Clay, 2011). Evans and co-workers (2006) found that clinical social workers show levels of stress and emotional exhaustion twice that of psychiatrists and three times that of the general population. Burnout levels of up to 40% have been reported in U.S. psychologists (Fortener, 1990). Results from surveys in the United Kingdom found that British clinical psychologists displayed even higher levels of emotional exhaustion, depersonalization and reduced personal accomplishment, three components of burnout, than their American colleagues (Cushway and Tyler, 1994). In addition, it was also found by these authors that personal doubt was a key stressor that appeared to correlate with burnout. Looking at indices of distress reactions less severe than burnout, Cushway and Tyler (1994) found in a survey of British clinical psychologists that 29.4% described themselves as "highly stressed."

Tables 1 and 2 below provide a summary review, from the studies above, of rates of compassion fatigue and burnout among different groups of professionals.

Table 1: Compassion fatigue in different professional groups	
Professional Group	**Approximate incidence of problem**
Health care workers in general	16-85%
Medical residents	54%
Emergency room nurses	33% meet criteria, 85% some symptoms in past week
Hospice workers	34%
Paramedics	25% and above

Table 2: Incidence of burnout in different groups	
Population	**Approximate incidence of problem**
Working adults in general	13-27.8%
Psychologists	Up to 40%
Mental health nurses/Occupational Therapists	54%
Pediatric oncologists	36%
Medicine interns/residents	34-69%
Medical Doctors in general	37.9-45.8%
Child care workers	50%
Clergy	40% mild to severe

PREDICTING CAREGIVER STRESS

The good news is that caregiver stress is somewhat predictable and thus at least partly preventable. We can look at caregiver personality traits, motivation and level of empathy and combine those with information about the work setting and clientele and come up with a fairly good guess about a person's risk level. Related to this is the question of what leads individuals to choose healthcare or counseling as a career. Does this career choice correlate with a particular type of personality? Does having certain personality traits make some professional helpers more vulnerable to distress or burnout? Some hypotheses have been offered regarding prevalent characteristics of therapists and helpers including:

- They have a strong desire to help others.
- They possess a good deal of idealism.
- They are optimistic about the ability of people to change.
- They are curious about human behavior.

Health care workers may be motivated in part by a desire to help others, or they may have a particular value system which is a good fit with this kind of work. This can be a mixed blessing, because higher levels of empathy have been shown to be linked to distress and compassion fatigue. Research suggests that certain personality types are more likely to experience caregiver stress or burnout. For example, the Type A behavior pattern, which is associated with being excessively conscientious, competitive, ambitious, and hard-driving, has been found to be a predictor of burnout in mental health workers (Rees & Cooper, 1992). It is not clear from empirical studies what personality characteristics or traits distinguish healthcare professionals from individuals in other careers, and which psychological characteristics are predictive of burnout and distress.

WHAT ARE SOME OF THE CAUSES OF CAREGIVER STRESS?

Although each of us will experience caregiver stress and burnout in our own way, there are certainly problems that we share. Sources of stress reported by a large number of mental health workers include feelings of inadequacy relative to one's own expectations, feeling pressure to cure clients, conflicts with other staff and problems with clients—especially those who are emotionally demanding or those who fail to improve. Evans et al. (2006) found that high job demands and not being valued for what one does are predictors of mental health worker burnout. Shinn et al. (1984) reported that lack of positive reinforcement or recognition for good work was reported by 44% of mental health professionals as a source of dissatisfaction or stress.

Moore and Cooper (1996) also point out that beyond the demands made by clients or organizations, the demands or expectations that mental health professionals place on themselves are also important predictors of caregiver stress and burnout. Pines and Maslach (1978) found that the longer individuals had worked in the mental health field the less successful they felt they were with people. The same researchers found that the higher the percentage of people with chronic problems in a mental health provider's caseload, the less job satisfaction they experienced. The length of time individuals had worked in the field was also a predictor of burnout, as was longer or more advanced training. Additional factors found to predict helper strain or distress include high numbers of emergency calls, interruptions in family life, difficulty dividing time between partner, family, and clients, unrealistic client expectations and therapist over-responsibility for people—family, friends and clients (Moore & Cooper, 1996).

Empathy and risk

"The capacity for compassion and empathy seems to be at the core of our ability to do the work and at the core of our ability to be wounded by the work."

—C. Figley

"Empathy is a double-edged sword; it is simultaneously your greatest asset and a point of real vulnerability."

—D.G. Larson

Most people who end up working in the helping professions report that they are highly empathetic people. Their empathy is what drew them into their field. It's also what can damage them through their work. Empathy is an obvious asset in a professional caregiver. However, there is a clear link between a high level of empathy and the development of compassion fatigue. Less empathetic individuals are at lower risk. They can still be extremely effective in the work they do, but their lower level of empathy proves to be protective.

> There is a clear link between a high level of empathy and the development of compassion fatigue. Less empathetic individuals are at lower risk.

Empathy which leads to impairment may involve putting both feet in the client's shoes instead of just one. In the process, the provider may lose objectivity and the ability to be both compassionate and helpful rather than just over-identifying with the client. Even Carl Rogers, whose approach highlighted therapist empathy, warmth and unconditional acceptance, cautioned against simple emotional shadowing (feeling bad because the client does).

Compassion fatigue can cause us to become less empathetic over time. Our compassionate connection erodes and we close ourselves off, often as protection against further wounding. We strive to be fully present for our clients, but this emotional involvement has consequences, particularly when the client is dealing with trauma. Our empathy ends up wounding us and making us more vulnerable to caregiver stress. It can lead to over-identification with our clients who suffer.

Over-identification may lead helpers to:

- Form an unhealthy bond
- Focus exclusively on the client's trauma
- Develop blurred boundaries
- Become enmeshed
- Try to rescue the client
- Advocate excessively for the client

Factors that **reduce** the risk of developing compassion fatigue:

- Reduced dose and intensity of secondary trauma exposure
- Older age
- Strong social support
- Impersonal trauma rather than interpersonal trauma
- Calm, non-anxious temperament

- Willingness to look for meaning in suffering
- Greater experience dealing with traumatized people
- Close connections with colleagues

Factors that **raise** the risk:

- The secondary trauma was an act of human cruelty rather than accidental or impersonal
- Longer exposure to the trauma of others
- Several other stressors occurring in the helper's life at the time of the secondary trauma exposure
- Personal trauma history (60% of helpers have a history of trauma)
- Lack of social support (this makes helpers four times more likely to experience compassion stress and two and a half times more likely to experience physical illness)
- Helper is anxiety-prone or habitually negative
- Idealistic expectations of ability to help others without consequence to self
- Working in isolation

Four areas to consider

There are four general areas we can look at to help assess someone's risk of developing compassion stress. They are:

Nature of the trauma

- Natural or human-caused
- Single event or multiple traumas
- Ethical or moral dilemmas involved
- Injury, abuse, mutilation or gore
- Developmental stage of person who experienced the trauma
- Duration, frequency and severity of the person's trauma
- Nature of the relationship between perpetrator and client

Client characteristics

- Demographics of the client and how close a match the person is to the helper's demographics
- Personality of the client
- Client's coping skills
- PTSD diagnosis in the person being helped

Therapist characteristics

- Similarity to client
- Personal beliefs and worldview
- Motivation for being a helping professional

- Training related to trauma and self-care
- History of trauma
- Stage of professional development
- Ability to use cognitive coping skills
- Willingness to seek support and supervision
- Expectations of professional self: realistic or unrealistic

Work setting

- Level of administrative support
- Resources available from the employer
- Provision of external sources of support
- Supervision and training related to compassion stress
- Flexibility and involvement of employer

RISK FACTORS

Knowing your own level of risk can help prevent and treat compassion stress. We suggest that helpers explore three main areas: the nature of the work, the traits of the clientele, and their own temperament. When looking at the nature of the work you can think about whether you have control over your schedule, how healthy your workplace is, how much support you receive and the level of concern that is expressed. As you consider the traits of the clientele you might assess how effective you feel as you work with people, look at your level of connection with your clients and whether you have balance and variety in your workday. It is helpful to reflect on your own temperament. Do you have meaningful connections with family and friends? Do you have fun? How are your coping skills?

RISK FACTORS

Assessing your own level of risk will help you modify how you approach your work and your self-care. Review these items to help determine your risk of compassion stress.

Factors that reduce risk:

____ I've had minimal exposure and intensity of secondary trauma.

____ I'm mid-career, not just starting out.

____ I have strong social support.

____ The suffering I've been exposed to is mainly impersonal trauma rather than interpersonal trauma.

____ Generally I have a calm, non-anxious temperament.

____ I'm willing to look for meaning in suffering.

____ I have experience dealing with traumatized people.

____ I have close connections with colleagues.

____ I feel well supported by my employer.

Factors that raise risk:

____ The trauma I've been exposed to has been acts of human cruelty rather than accidental or impersonal.

____ I've had longer exposure to the trauma of others.

____ I have had several other stressors occurring in my life at the time of my secondary trauma exposure.

____ I have a personal trauma history.

____ I lack social support.

____ I'm somewhat anxiety-prone or habitually negative.

____ I have idealistic expectations of my ability to help others without consequence to myself.

____ I tend to work in isolation.

____ The suffering I've heard about has often involved multiple traumas.

____ I have heard a lot of stories with injury, abuse or gory details.

____ Sometimes I really identify strongly with my clients.

____ I worry that my clients have inadequate coping skills.

CHECKLIST

ASSESSING RISK

It's helpful to figure out what your level of risk might be. Caregiver stress can impact people in many different professions. Go through this list of questions to determine if you are at risk.

PERSONAL HISTORY

Consider your own personality style and history as you go through this checklist.

____ I have a lot of empathy.

____ I don't have a very strong support system.

____ I am an anxious person and have trouble staying calm.

____ I'm new in the field, not very experienced dealing with suffering people.

____ It's hard for me to find meaning in suffering.

____ I've had a lot of stressors in my life at the time I've worked with traumatized people.

____ I have a history of trauma in my own life.

____ People think I'm negative or pessimistic.

____ I think I ought to be able to help people effectively.

____ Sometimes I feel like I have a lot in common with the people I'm helping.

____ It's hard for me to change my thinking about suffering.

____ I like to think I can figure things out myself and I hesitate to seek supervision or support.

WORK SETTING

As you look at this list of questions think about your work setting, either at present or in the past when you worked in another job dealing with people who had trauma and suffering in their lives.

____ I don't think my employer takes compassion stress very seriously.

____ My employer doesn't do much to make me feel supported.

____ Other people at my workplace deal with these reactions too.

____ We haven't had much training in compassion stress.

____ I wish my supervisor would be more in touch with these issues and provide more effective support to me.

____ It would be great if my employer were more flexible and involved.

____ Sometimes I work with people who I have some similarities to.

____ I have worked with people who have been through trauma and may have PTSD.

____ There are people I work with who have suffered, but don't have very effective coping skills.

____ I've heard a lot of stories that disturb me.

____ Some of the details I've heard from people upset me.

PHYSICIAN, HEAL THYSELF!

We have seen from the previous section how common and how impairing some of these problems can be for health care providers. So it would seem obvious that for individuals working in such a demanding and stressful field as professional care giving, there is a great need to practice good self-care. Unfortunately, all too often those of us in the helping professions put ourselves at the bottom of our own lists.

Why do caregivers neglect self care?

Many helping professionals take great care of others, but aren't as diligent about taking care of themselves. It could be that we don't place a very high priority on keeping ourselves well and healthy. We may also deny our own challenges, which can lead us to avoid dealing with them. We may not always practice what we preach and are guilty of a "do as I say, not as I do" stance, in that we encourage clients to seek balance and look after themselves when dealing with stressful situations, but we may not give the same attention to this when we ourselves are struggling.

A few reasons for this disparity:

- You may not recognize your own level of distress, because you don't give yourself enough time for reflection.
- Distress may be manifested in disguised ways (headaches leading to a search for a physical or medical explanation rather than a psychological one).
- You may make a false attribution about what is going on or what you really need (decide you just need a vacation rather than looking at the bigger picture of what needs to change).
- Even while recognizing the need for self-care, because of limited time and multiple demands on this time, you may decide that improved self-care is simply not feasible.
- You may hold beliefs which get in the way of appropriately prioritizing self-care activities. (You may think, "I should spend my free time reading up on improvements in treatments for my clients rather than taking a yoga course for me").

Rates of depression, stress and psychiatric morbidity are very high in caregivers, as can be seen in Table 3.

Table 3: Incidence of stress and psychiatric morbidity in different professional groups		
Group	Significant stress	Psychiatric morbidity
Psychologists	36% stressed, 20-29.4% highly stressed	
Mental health social workers	Levels of stress and emotional exhaustion 3 times general population and twice that of psychiatrists	
Therapists		60% psychiatric disorder at some time in career 1 in 4 have suicide ideation, 1 in 16 attempt suicide
MDs		22.3% psychiatric disorder
Family practitioners		27% clinically or borderline depressed
Surgeons		1.5-3 times rate of suicidal ideation of general population

However, a large percentage of those who suffer do not reach out to peers or seek professional help. This may be because of dysfunctional beliefs regarding the need or appropriateness. Typical examples of these kinds of dysfunctional beliefs include:

- Not recognizing the severity of their distress
- Not giving themselves permission to seek help
- Feeling that since they are helpers they should be able to help themselves
- Experiencing a sense of shame, failure or stigma if they acknowledge having issues

Norcross and Guy (2007) list the following as the most likely reasons mental health professionals do not seek professional help:

- Feelings of embarrassment or humiliation
- Doubts regarding the efficacy of therapy
- Previous negative experiences with therapy
- Feelings of superiority hindering ability to identify own need for help
- Complicating practical factors such as knowing many of the professionals in their geographical area

While we acknowledge the legitimacy of concerns a professional seeking help from colleagues might have about how he or she might be seen by colleagues, it is worth considering that we should actively challenge the implication that providers who are in therapy are the ones who are impaired. In fact, they are acting in their clients' and in their own best interests. We should be more concerned about the about health care providers who need help but don't seek it. So if you are reading this book and recognizing that you might be struggling with some distressed feelings, we'd encourage you to consider a much greater focus on self-care. If a part of this were to involve some peer or professional help, you might have had some reluctance to take this step. It would be worth checking if you have any beliefs that get in the way of doing this such as:

- I shouldn't have any psychological problems
- If I do, I should not admit to them
- I can't go into therapy, because therapists (caregivers) should be able to solve their own problems

Failure to take adequate care of oneself may result in: (1) incapacitating personal distress, (2) impaired relationships, (3) moral and spiritual issues and (4) impaired professional behavior including ethical violations.

Personal distress

Individuals experiencing personal distress which rises to the level of burnout or compassion fatigue, or remains at a milder and less impairing level, where the distress may be more situational or transient, may experience problems in a number of different categories. In some cases, the severity of these symptoms may indicate the presence of a psychological disorder. (As previously stated, a key determinant of how significant and problematic these indicators of distress are is to ascertain if any of the above represent a departure from the individual's baseline functioning.)

Personal distress due to failure of self-care has essentially the same signs and symptoms as those of caregiver stress and burnout. They include physical, somatic, emotional and behavioral problems, as well as cognitive or attitudinal problems.

Relationship issues

Research has shown that counselors and caregivers in general have high levels of divorce and relationship problems (greater than in the general population). Clearly, working in this field is costly in terms of the impact of this kind of work on non-work relationships. It would be unrealistic to expect that there will not be a bleedover from the stresses of dealing with, for example, highly suicidal individuals, terminally ill clients or victims of abuse. Often healthcare providers don't want to burden their partners (or families and friends) with their concerns or sources of distress, but this doesn't mean that their stressed state does not have an impact on these others who undoubtedly know that something is wrong, but not exactly what it is, when there is a failure to communicate. Alternatively, they (partners, family and friends) may well feel burdened if too much is shared. This is a situation ripe for relationship impairment and many of the behaviors listed previously under personal distress will have a significant impact on relationships (for example, distrust of others or irritability) with partners, family and friends.

Moral distress

Value conflicts or questioning of meaning can be a big issue when individuals become burned out. One frequent feature of burnout is a sense of cynicism, which may represent a changing moral compass from earlier altruism and a sense of hope, to one of blame and lack of compassion. In such a context ethical violations are possible and clients may be manipulated or used in ways which spring from a moral decline or loss of moral standards. Burned out caregivers may cease to find any meaning in what they do and perhaps more generally in their lives. This clearly represents a dangerous situation in terms of demoralization, suicidal potential and other issues.

Impaired professional behavior

The signs and symptoms of personal distress outlined previously can have ramifications in the arena of behavior and attitude towards clients and colleagues as well as friends and family members. Apart from morally compromised behavior, other non-therapeutic behaviors may occur as a direct consequence of a therapist's level of stress, such as avoidance of clients, long delays in returning calls, a sarcastic or cynical attitude, failure to implement treatment or other procedures correctly and a general non-adherence to acceptable professional standards.

RECOGNIZING HOW DISTRESS IMPACTS YOU

Have you experienced any indicators of personal distress?

Yes _____ No _____

If so, which indicators?

_____

_____

_____

_____

_____

_____

_____

_____

Have you ever felt, even briefly, that your work was impaired or negatively impacted?

Yes _____ No _____

If so, how?

_____

_____

_____

_____

_____

_____

_____

_____

Chapter 2
Put on Your Own Oxygen Mask First

Flight attendants remind us to put on our own oxygen masks before we help others, meaning secure your own safety before you try to help anyone else. But, on the ground, so many care providers don't or won't take the time to tend to their own emotional needs, a failure that might very well impact their work with clients.

We would guess that dysfunctional beliefs about seeking help or admitting there are problems probably exist in many health care providers. The good news is that we can effectively combat our own dysfunctional thinking and behavior, as we will see later in the Interventions section.

Instead of "I shouldn't have any psychological problems," we would encourage you to think something like:

> It is not having negative emotions or stress reactions (including compassion fatigue, burnout or transient work-related stress response) that is the problem. These will occur because I am human. It is how I manage them that is important, and I owe it to myself to do the best I can do for myself in this regard.

TARGETS FOR INTERVENTION

To understand how health care providers may be at risk for both burnout and high levels of distress it may be helpful to provide a conceptualization or model of distress in caregivers which then helps us to consider appropriate targets for intervention.

A number of different issues can contribute to distress reactions in healthcare professionals. The confluence of factors, which may predict distress in a particular individual at a particular time, will now be examined. It is hypothesized that the following factors may play a role in the development of the negative emotional and behavioral outcomes described previously:

- Situational triggers at work, including both client-related and non client-related work stressors
- Psychological characteristics of the health care provider
- Expectations and beliefs of the health care provider
- Personal coping style, skills and resources of the individual
- Levels of non-work stress
- The degree to which the professional training received equips the individual deal with these stressors
- The presence or absence of staff support systems to reduce or alleviate these problems

Using the above analysis we could predict maximum levels of distress where a health care provider:

- Has a large caseload with many challenging clients
- Has unrealistic beliefs regarding these clients, treatment, or himself or herself as a therapist or care provider
- Works in a very autocratic agency, which makes many demands on the individual but provides little reward or staff support and fails to prioritize staff satisfaction or fulfillment
- Has received little or no training in coping with the emotional reactions triggered by working in the health care field
- Has little emotional resilience and poor problem solving or coping skills
- Has a great deal of additional non-work stress in his or her life

Conversely, we might expect that low levels of stress would be found in providers who have few of the above factors present. Successful interventions and preventive efforts to reduce distress should target each of these areas. Specifically, the following may become targets for intervention:

- Reducing or better managing client-related and other work stressors
- Modifying and revising dysfunctional beliefs and expectations of therapists
- Facilitating better agency support and supervision for individuals dealing with challenging cases and situations
- Encouraging and promoting better training for providers in management of their own emotional reactions
- Helping to develop better coping resources and problem-solving skills leading to a greater sense of self-efficacy

Client-related stressors

The following client situations can provide potential trigger situations for distress or frustration in care providers:

- Highly suicidal individuals
- Chronically depressed clients
- Angry and volatile individuals
- Noncompliant clients
- Terminally ill clients
- Individuals with chronic illnesses including pain disorders
- Highly anxious clients
- Demanding or dependent clients

IDENTIFYING YOUR CLIENT-RELATED STRESSORS

Which types of clients do you sometimes or often find it hard to work with?

_____

_____

_____

_____

Which elicit some stress responses in you? _____

_____

_____

_____

What client situations are difficult for you to deal with? _____

_____

_____

_____

Why do you think you might have this difficulty?_____

_____

_____

_____

ARE YOU AT RISK?

Given what we have learned about the risks of developing significant caregiver distress reactions, we will outline a model of caretaker distress and propose some possible solutions. Leahy (2001) theorizes that there are certain core needs that some therapists appear to have and which motivate them. They can also be a recipe for distress if they remain unsatisfied.

These include:

- A need for approval, respect and admiration
- A desire for control, competence or power
- A tendency to excessive self-sacrifice or co-dependency
- A need for the reinforcement provided by emotional voyeurism
- A desire to be perfect with very high standards being set for themselves and their clients
- A need for superiority over others, which is enshrined in an all-powerful, overly-directive therapist role
- An aspiration to understand oneself better through therapy and training

Clearly, many of these are dysfunctional in that they will conflict with the reality of day-to-day situations faced by therapists.

Though the motivational factors may have been complex, there is high likelihood that you along with most people in the care giving field wished to effect change or help others.

It is worthwhile to reflect on the choice to enter this field as it can illuminate both the rewards hoped for (and hopefully received, at least in part) and also indicate where you may be vulnerable to distress, burnout or compassion fatigue because of those same factors.

EXERCISE

IDENTIFYING REWARDS AND POTENTIAL REWARDS FROM YOUR WORK

What rewards **could** you receive from the kind of work you do? _____

_____

What rewards do you **actually** receive from your work? _____

_____

What motivated you to choose the work you do? Think back to when you decided to make health care your choice of career. Try to recall what the factors in your choice were.

_____

_____

_____

_____

If you are having difficulty answering this question, do you think it could have been:

• An interest in human behavior or problems

• A desire to help others

• A feeling you could make a difference

• A quest for power or status

• Predicted financial or other rewards (increased self esteem)

BELIEF SYSTEMS OF HELPERS

The other side of having a deep desire to help struggling humanity, or more specifically, individuals we encounter in our work who have serious problems, is that we may often be frustrated, anxious or sad when we cannot or do not reduce their suffering. This may be because factors outside of our control interfere with the achieving such outcomes (some illnesses are incurable, some pain is intractable, some clients may remain in the bad situation they are in because the fear of change is too great). Not acknowledging this, or understanding it at an intellectual level but not modifying our expectations and beliefs accordingly, can set us up for anguish and disappointment.

Wanting to help everyone we encounter professionally is a noble aspiration, but it is just that, an aspiration, and should never be an imperative or demand. In addition, conditional beliefs such as "If I can help clients, I can the feel good about myself" with the implication that the opposite would also be true; "If I can't help clients, I cannot feel good about myself," need to be modified as they are traps.

Albert Ellis, a famous psychotherapist, spoke of the danger of "musturbation" and this is an example of this. Any readers who are or have become aware of the operation of these kinds of rules may need to challenge and question these as outlined later in this book. Many of our belief systems, of course, derive from family learning and it can be instructive to look at family of origin experiences which are related to the issues of beliefs and expectations of caregivers. Health care providers often come from families where parents, siblings or other family members also work in the field. This can create a certain pressure (external and internal) to (a) enter the field and (b) be successful in this career. It is understandable then that individuals with this family background may have difficulty accepting that they are suffering from burnout, compassion fatigue or even distress in general related to work.

Additionally, there may be certain family values which have powerful effects on an individual. For example, someone might have heard as child that "Helping others is better than attending to one's own needs," "It is better to give than receive" or "You will always feel good about yourself if you help others." These can echo and affect individuals in their later work as a care provider. Are you aware of any such rules or assumptions in your family growing up and have they hindered you in any way as an adult?

Much of what is being described here can be seen as involving certain ways of thinking which a cognitive behavioral model (to be described later) posits are important determining factors in emotional and behavioral problems. The beliefs or thoughts of professional helpers can be broken down into:

1. Beliefs or expectations concerning clients
2. Beliefs or expectations for themselves
3. More general beliefs about work

Examples of dysfunctional beliefs concerning clients might include:

- My clients should not be difficult, resistant or challenging
- They should work as hard as I do to make treatment work

- All my client sessions should be as the textbooks describe
- I should never be disrespected or criticized by a client
- Clients should be motivated to change and to fully engage in treatment
- I should be loved and admired by my clients

Examples of dysfunctional beliefs concerning ourselves might include:

- I must be successful with all my clients
- If I am not successful in alleviating clients' problems, I can't feel good about myself
- I should not dislike any of my clients
- I must always have good judgment as a professional
- I should have all the answers
- I should not have any emotional reactions myself and, if I do, I should control them and never show this to clients or colleagues
- My worth as person is dependent on my job performance
- I must have things the way I want them
- I will be seen as weak if I ask for help
- Other people should see things my way
- I must be perceived as totally competent

> It is useful to examine the underlying expectations, beliefs, and assumptions of care providers when experiencing work-related distress. Thinking patterns similar to those above should be identified and then dealt with effectively using cognitive behavioral methods, as will be described later.

Expectations for our work, of course, may also be problematic in that we come to expect that success derives from hard work alone. For example, when we are in graduate school, careful and sustained study leads to good academic outcomes (good exam results). Does it work this way in the practice of health care?

Because there are factors that are uncontrollable despite our diligence and efforts to influence outcomes, we only have limited control in creating positive outcomes or even in receiving appreciation for our efforts. Some individuals recognize this and have realistic expectations; some don't and become casualties.

Lack of Organizational Support

Case supervision, which constitutes possibly the best form of organizational or peer support, is often inadequate or non-existent. Within agencies it is often set up only to meet the requirements of the state or the agency itself. It is rare for an agency to routinely make peer, group or individual supervision available for caregivers dealing with difficult or challenging cases. Yet this would be time well spent and, most likely, be cost-effective in that it would probably improve client outcomes. In addition it would show recognition of the distress and strain experienced by staff members, which would lead to a greater sense of being appreciated among health care providers and increase worker satisfaction.

Administrative support might come in the form of setting up supervision and team meetings, sending individuals to training sessions on this topic or bringing in speakers to provide onsite, staff-wide training in some of these issues. Additionally, organizing staff retreats with workshops focusing not on learning more about certain disorders and therapy, but rather on helping employees themselves by providing stress-reducing activities in a relaxing setting would be conducive to distress-management.

> Regrettably, in many agencies, staff members are often so overloaded with clients and mandatory meetings that there is no time for the type of support activities outlined here, and this can be a recipe for burnout and distress.

In private practice, where a provider is paid only for billable hours involving client contact, it may be a low priority to organize something like the above, but the benefits of having even occasional staffing and supervision sessions with colleagues inside or outside the practice, as a means of dealing with some of these issues, should not be overlooked.

Since as we have seen previously that organizational factors can be risks for compassion fatigue or burnout, organizations themselves could help to allay effects in many ways. Facilitating enriching peer or supervisory relationships would prevent depletion and demoralization. However, many agencies or organizations provide little in the way of support for individuals with work-related issues. Poor monitoring of, and intervention with, staff members often means the individual is left isolated and without help. When this situation is combined with personal beliefs rendering the individual unlikely to ask for help, it's a recipe for unnecessary distress. Agencies which create a climate of appreciation, support, and attention to professional development and seek feedback on personal fulfillment tend to be places where, all other things being equal, individuals will experience fewer of the negative reactions enumerated previously. However, these appear to be the exceptions. Maslach and Leiter (1997) claim that, "burnout is not a problem of the people themselves but of the social environment in which the people work." They indicate that "breakdown of community" is an important factor in determining burnout. However this breakdown is created, organizations, agencies and peers can be a part of the solution.

ASSESSING ORGANIZATIONAL SUPPORT

What does your organization do towards professional development and peer support or stress reduction?

_____

_____

_____

_____

What might your organization do in this regard?

_____

_____

_____

_____

Does your organization organize training or forums to discuss these issues?

_____

_____

_____

_____

What about your professional organization? What is available from them (training or resources)?

_____

_____

_____

_____

Training inadequacies

Many cognitive behavior therapy texts, especially those which deal with challenging cases (Beck et al., 2003; Beck, 2005; Layden et al., 1993; Leahy, 2001), devote time and attention to the topic of therapist reactions, and it could be argued that clinical and professional training courses should also focus more on these issues. In examining workshops and seminars presented at national mental health conferences for professionals, this topic is usually conspicuous by its absence. As a result of this, and the lack of attention given to this topic in training, one is left with the idea that caregiver distress is really not a problem or is a low priority issue. Consequently, any professional helper experiencing some of the problems outlined in this book may well be ashamed or embarrassed to talk about these issues or ask for help or support and may end up believing (falsely) that no one else feels this way.

In the later parts of the book, some suggestions will be made for institutional changes which would help with this problem of inadequate training and lack of agency support in dealing with these issues. At this point it could be said that individuals in charge of organizing or providing clinical training or supervision for health care professionals should prioritize this issue.

In supervising therapists we (the authors) tend to focus on supervisees' emotional status vis-à-vis certain challenging cases, as well as helping them develop better conceptualization and intervention skills. It is obvious that a supervisee's emotional reactions will affect the degree to which his or her therapeutic endeavors are likely to be effective.

A recent study of therapists in supervision during cognitive therapy training found that the trainees' ratings of their own competence was influenced strongly by their emotional state and stress levels (Bennett-Levy & Beedie, 2007). In addition, the type of supervision described above, which focuses on both client issues and the therapist's reactions, can greatly reduce personal work-related stress, as well as fine-tuning therapists' clinical skills. We know from our own experience how invaluable and protective of one's well-being such training and supervision can be.

ASSESSING HOW MUCH TRAINING
YOU HAVE HAD IN SELF-CARE

Have you had training since graduating?_____

_____

_____

_____

_____

_____

_____

_____

Was it beneficial?_____

_____

_____

_____

_____

_____

_____

_____

_____

If you did not receive training, would you have benefitted from this? _____

_____

_____

_____

_____

_____

_____

_____

Chapter 3
Cognitive Behavioral Model of Provider Distress

The cognitive behavioral model (Beck et al., 1979) which has been demonstrated to be effective in helping a variety of client groups, such as those with mood and anxiety disorders, is also equally applicable to the provider.

The cognitive behavioral model theorizes that:

> The cognitive behavioral model is equally applicable to the provider and the client.

1. Cognitive events and processes significantly influence emotions and behavior.
2. Perception and cognition mediate the effects of situations with regard to emotional and behavioral consequences.
3. Modification of cognition leads to emotional and behavioral change.

The extension of the CBT model can be seen in the diagram below. A more detailed analysis of the components of the model as applied to professionals is outlined further on.

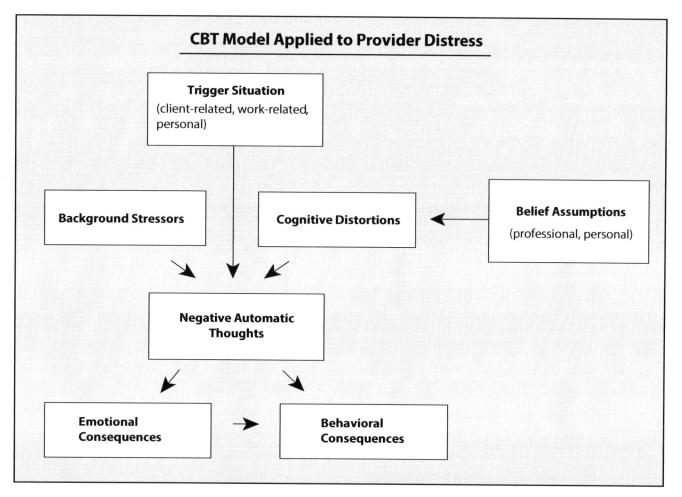

TRIGGER SITUATIONS

The triggers (situations which can precipitate emotional and behavioral reactions) for health practitioners may include client or therapy-related events and/or other work-related situations (organizational or administrative).

Examples of client-related triggers include:

- Dealing with a very demanding client who makes frequent requests for extra, emergency sessions or telephones regularly in crisis
- Working with a highly suicidal or hopeless client
- Attempting to do therapy with a "resistant" client who challenges the therapist every step of the way
- Working with emotionally charged issues in a client, such as child sexual abuse, rape or violence

Examples of work-related stressors might be:

- Being overwhelmed by paperwork
- Being assigned too many cases or a large number of difficult cases
- Role conflict or role ambiguity
- Interpersonal conflict at work
- Professional isolation

BACKGROUND STRESSORS

Background stressors, which might lower the threshold for emotional and cognitive reactions in particular situations, can involve any events inside or outside work which can create distress for providers, such as a change of job, increase in work hours, family problems and financial difficulties.

BELIEFS

This refers to general assumptions, rules or beliefs, which individuals adopt and which profoundly influence how experiences are viewed and interpreted.

Key dysfunctional beliefs relating to work as a health care provider might include:

- I have to be successful with all my clients all the time.
- I must always have good sessions with my clients.
- I should not dislike any of my clients.
- I should not feel any negative emotions related to clients or therapy.
- I should not ask for advice or support from colleagues or get professional help myself.
- My clients should always respect and like me.
- People I try to help should not be difficult and resistant.
- If I extend myself to help clients, they ought to be motivated to change and reward me for my efforts.

More general dysfunctional beliefs relating to work might include:

- I must always be totally competent and in control.
- It is terrible to be disapproved of or criticized.
- Life in the workplace should be fair and just.
- My worth as a person is dependent on my job performance.

COGNITIVE DISTORTIONS

Cognitive distortions are information processing biases or thinking errors, which are influenced by beliefs and generate negative automatic thoughts. In mental health practice the following distortions might be seen:

- *All or nothing thinking:* Seeing things as black or white. For example, a therapist thinking he or she is a total failure as a therapist based on the fact that some clients are not improving.
- *Overgeneralizing:* One negative event is seen as a general pattern. For example, an assumption is made by the therapist that since one of his or her clients is unhappy with treatment then none of his or her clients is satisfied with the therapy being provided.
- *Mental filter:* Seeing only the negative aspects of a situation and filtering out the positives. For example, the provider sees only the fact that a client has had a setback and fails to recognize how stable the client has been recently and how the setback was handled by the individual.
- *Mind-reading:* Assuming one knows what someone is thinking. For example, it is assumed that since a client failed to keep an appointment this means that the client thinks the therapy or therapist is unhelpful.

AUTOMATIC THOUGHTS

Automatic thoughts are specific thoughts, images or memories related to a specific precipitating situation and are often reflexive in nature. These can be negative in tone and often will have adverse emotional consequences. Negative automatic thoughts related to a specific client situation might include the following:

- There is no progress.
- I am not helping this client at all.
- If the client is angry or critical, I am not handling things properly.
- The client is resisting me and doesn't want to change or improve.
- This person's situation is so realistically terrible that there is nothing I can do to help.
- I get all the difficult cases like this one.

Automatic thoughts experienced by providers related to non-client situations might include the following:

- My supervisor or colleagues are totally unsupportive of me.
- I will never get this paperwork done.

- Everybody is dumping on me.
- Why do I bother when I get so few rewards, financial or otherwise?

EMOTIONAL AND BEHAVIORAL REACTIONS

Emotional reactions may include anger, frustration, anxiety, irritability, sadness and dysphoria. Behavioral reactions may involve a range of unhealthy or maladaptive behaviors to deal with the stress encountered with clients or work in general. These may include:

- Working longer and longer hours
- Isolating oneself from family, friends and colleagues
- Overeating, drinking or using drugs

In addition there may a tendency to act or behave towards clients in a way which becomes anti-therapeutic and involves a poor standard of care, such as:

- Withdrawing from the client in session
- Becoming much less active in session
- Providing support rather than the more problem-focused therapy the therapist customarily practices
- Displaying irritable behavior towards the client
- Procrastination expressed in not returning phone calls and being chronically late for sessions

EXAMPLES OF PROVIDER REACTIONS

In the next several pages a number of examples of how this model can explain a provider's reactions will be given.

Example 1

Several years ago I (JL) had a "light bulb moment" related to my professional life, which demonstrated clearly the critical role which cognitions can play in the distress experienced in working as a mental health professional. I was attending a workshop on cognitive reappraisal therapy, one of a number of cognitive behavioral models. I volunteered to be a client in a role-play with the presenter. I was instructed to think of a recent experience involving a negative emotional shift. A day earlier I had learned that a client of mine, who I had been seeing in therapy for over a year, had had a major relapse and been hospitalized. I was still experiencing some distress concerning this development during the workshop. When I described the situation (the client's relapse and subsequent hospitalization) to my "therapist" (the presenter), the following interchange took place:

Presenter as therapist: What feelings do you have about this situation?

Me: Guilt, anxiety.

Presenter as therapist: What thoughts are you having about this situation? What does it mean to you?

Me: That my therapy wasn't successful.

Presenter as therapist: And if that was true, what would that mean?

Me: That I am not a good therapist.

Presenter as therapist: And if that were true, what would that mean?

Me: That I am inadequate.

Presenter as therapist: As a therapist?

Me: Yes, and as a person too.

The "therapist" then went back and summarized the chain of assumptions implicit in my moving from the factual knowledge that my client had relapsed to my belief that I was inadequate as a person. These were:

- If this client has relapsed, then my therapy was not successful.
- If my therapy was not successful, then I am not a good therapist.
- If I am not a good therapist, then I am inadequate as a person.

I was startled to discover how irrational and dysfunctional my thinking was, especially since I was a practicing cognitive therapist, who helped my clients daily with their irrational thoughts! That obviously did not automatically protect me from having irrational and dysfunctional thoughts myself. In addition, I had always seen myself as a therapist who was well-adjusted, did not get overly-involved emotionally, lose perspective or have unrealistic expectations regarding myself and my clients. Since this "wake-up call," I have made it a point to closely monitor my own cognitions and feelings in therapy situations.

Further, in supervising novice therapists, I have encouraged them to examine the cognitive and emotional effects on themselves of the therapeutic impasses or difficulties they report in supervision. They are further urged to use cognitive interventions on their own distorted thinking, which is often linked to negative emotional reactions, as the cognitive behavioral model would predict.

In the example given above, the complex interaction of trigger situations, thoughts and negative feelings can be seen. There are clearly a number of levels of cognition involved in the overall reaction. Specifically, there are:

- Negative automatic thoughts related to the situation of the client relapse ("This therapy wasn't successful")
- Cognitive distortions or information processing biases which included mental filter and personalization
- Dysfunctional beliefs which included (a) professional beliefs ("I am not a good therapist") and, (b) personal beliefs ("I am inadequate")

This example fits with the cognitive model presented previously and illustrates it in a clear and understandable way. The other components in the diagram shown earlier are behavior and background stress. The cognitive and emotional reactions outlined in the previous example might have also led to behaviors such as the provision of inferior therapy, attempts to overcompensate by doing too much for other clients or maladaptive behavior outside of work such as overeating, irritability and withdrawal.

Background stress, such as concerns and worries related to health and family, could also have lowered the threshold for dysfunctional responding, both emotional and cognitive.

Example 2

It may be helpful to imagine yourself being in this hypothetical situation. A client is referred to you by a colleague who notes that there may be some "borderline tendencies." Preparing for your first interview with this new client, you might notice some feelings of anxiety or irritation possibly linked to negative thoughts such as, "the client will be very angry, will be difficult to treat, will be resistant and challenge me at every step. It is not fair that I get all the difficult cases."

> It is important for therapists learn to take care of themselves emotionally by developing skills to detect and deal with the emotional challenges faced every day in the field they have chosen.

These automatic thoughts might in turn be maintained by underlying beliefs such as, "clients should always treat me well and be compliant and easy," or "life in the workplace should be fair." As a result of the emotional and cognitive reactions described above, your behavior toward the client might be different from your normal therapy behavior, in that you may be more distant, act defensively or become overly vigilant with this client. These behaviors may in turn trigger some "borderline" or anti-therapeutic behavior in the client, if he or she perceives you to be uncaring, untrustworthy or disinterested. This set of thoughts and expectations can have a damaging effect on the therapy itself and also triggers a lot of pre-emptive distress in the therapist.

Challenging and modifying such thoughts to something like: "I will have to wait and see what, if any, borderline features this client has; meanwhile, I will concentrate on my two goals for this first session which are to identify problems and targets, and to develop initial rapport with the client" would reduce the anxiety and irritation experienced and also facilitate more effective therapy.

It is important for therapists learn to take care of themselves emotionally by developing skills to detect and deal with the emotional challenges faced every day in the field they have chosen. In doing so, not only will their levels of emotional distress be lower, but they will in all likelihood be more effective providers too, as it appears obvious that such reactions can interfere with the provision of "good" treatment. The rest of this book will offer some practical tools to assist therapists in reducing stress and distress in the workplace.

Chapter 4
Detection

The metaphor of road journey is an interesting and helpful way to consider the issues of provider burnout and compassion fatigue. This next section deals with detection which can aid both intervention and prevention. To avoid breaking down on the road, oil and other factors for our car's drivability need to be checked before setting out and during the journey. Attention will need to be paid to any warning signals of potential problems inside and outside the car. Likewise, noting how we are functioning and recognizing early signs of distress will be a vital part of improved self-care and staying on course.

SELF-ASSESSMENT USING THE PROQOL

You may need some guidance and direction as you try to determine how your work is impacting you. There may be confusion about symptoms and how to interpret them. Sometimes it's hard to tell the difference between compassion fatigue, vicarious traumatization, burnout and stress.

In the 1990's people began using the Compassion Fatigue Self-Test. This was basically a checklist of symptoms that helpers could endorse to get a sense of the presence or absence of symptoms. Charles Figley, PhD, is credited with its development. Figley was affiliated with Florida State University during the 1990's and is widely known as the father of the compassion fatigue movement. This instrument was handed off to Beth Hudnall-Stamm, PhD, at Idaho State University for further development.

The ProQOL is now the most widely used evidence-based assessment of compassion fatigue, compassion satisfaction and burnout. The ProQOL is well validated and available for free public use with no copyright concerns. It can be administered online or on paper, with groups or individuals. There is a choice of wording for several of the items, which means that it can be tailored to meet the needs of any group of professionals who take it. The website (www.proqol. org) has an exhaustive bibliography of over 1,000 entries. There is also a comprehensive manual online that gives all kinds of scoring information and additional details.

ProQOL
The ProQOL manual gives some interesting information about scores. Here are a few highlights:

- People who have been in the helping professions longer seem to get better scores. (This could be because they have developed coping skills and resiliency through the years. It's also possible that people with more traumatic exposure fallout may have left the field earlier. That attrition could skew the results in such a way that the remaining professionals look hardier. . .sort of a "survival of the fittest").
- People over 35 have better scores.
- Non-whites get slightly worse scores.

- Females have slightly worse scores.
- Scores improve slightly with higher income. This could be due to several factors: people with higher salaries may be farther away from the front lines of client care and be more likely to be administrators or supervisors. It's also possible that people remaining in the field longer (who tend to have better scores) make more money. It also seems likely that folks who make more money may feel more appreciated by their employer, which could offset the downside of working as a helping professional.
- Working with traumatized children leads to worse scores. Most adults feel a sense of responsibility to protect children and are affected when children suffer. We often view children as being innocent (true), but we may blame adults, at least in part, for the traumatic situations they experience (maybe true, often not).
- Teachers typically have high scores on the compassion satisfaction scale. The goal of teachers is to impart information, not to resolve children's experiences with suffering and trauma. Teachers often work surrounded by other teachers and have a natural support system. Teachers also often have resources to whom to refer troubled children (school counselors, school social workers, therapists, children's protective services).

Taking the ProQOL

The ProQOL is the most widely used measure of compassion satisfaction, burnout and vicarious trauma. Take your time as you read and respond to the questions. Consider the impact of your work over the past 30 days. The scoring explanation will guide you on how to score your answers and how to interpret the results. For more details about the instrument or scoring, refer to the manual at http://www.proqol.org/ProQOl_Test_Manuals.html.

PROFESSIONAL QUALITY OF LIFE SCALE (PROQOL)

COMPASSION SATISFACTION AND COMPASSION FATIGUE
(PROQOL) VERSION 5 (2009)

When you *[help]* people you have direct contact with their lives. As you may have found, your compassion for those you *[help]* can affect you in positive and negative ways. Below are some-questions about your experiences, both positive and negative, as a *[helper]*. Consider each of the following questions about you and your current work situation. Select the number that honestly reflects how frequently you experienced these things in the *last 30 days*.

1=Never	2=Rarely	3=Sometimes	4=Often	5=Very often

_____ 1. I am happy.

_____ 2. I am preoccupied with more than one person I *[help]*.

_____ 3. I get satisfaction from being able to *[help]* people.

_____ 4. I feel connected to others.

_____ 5. I jump or am startled by unexpected sounds.

_____ 6. I feel invigorated after working with those I *[help]*.

_____ 7. I find it difficult to separate my personal life from my life as a *[helper]*.

_____ 8. I am not as productive at work because I am losing sleep over traumatic experiences of a person I *[help]*.

_____ 9. I think that I might have been affected by the traumatic stress of those I *[help]*.

_____10. I feel trapped by my job as a *[helper]*.

_____11. Because of my *[helping]*, I have felt "on edge" about various things.

_____12. I like my work as a *[helper]*.

_____13. I feel depressed because of the traumatic experiences of the people I *[help]*.

_____14. I feel as though I am experiencing the trauma of someone I have *[helped]*.

_____15. I have beliefs that sustain me.

_____16. I am pleased with how I am able to keep up with *[helping]* techniques and protocols.

_____17. I am the person I always wanted to be.

_____18. My work makes me feel satisfied.

_____19. I feel worn out because of my work as a *[helper]*.

_____20. I have happy thoughts and feelings about those I *[help]* and how I could help them.

_____21. I feel overwhelmed because my case [work] load seems endless.

_____22. I believe I can make a difference through my work.

_____23. I avoid certain activities or situations because they remind me of frightening experience of the people I *[help]*.

_____24. I am proud of what I can do to *[help]*.

_____25. As a result of my *[helping]*, I have intrusive, frightening thoughts.

_____26. I feel "bogged down" by the system.

_____27. I have thoughts that I am a "success" as a *[helper]*.

_____28. I can't recall important parts of my work with trauma victims.

_____29. I am a very caring person.

_____30. I am happy that I chose to do this work.

WHAT IS MY SCORE AND WHAT DOES IT MEAN?

In this section, you will score your test so you understand the interpretation for you. To find your score on each section, total the questions listed on the left and then find your score in the table on the right of the section.

Compassion Satisfaction Scale

Copy your rating on each of these questions on to this table and add them up. When you have added then up you can find your score on the table to the right.

3._____
6._____
12._____
16._____
18._____
20._____
22._____
24._____
27._____
30._____

Total:_____

The sum of my Compassion Satisfaction questions is	So My Score Equals	And my Compassion Satisfaction level is
22 or less	43 or less	Low
Between 23 and 41	Around 50	Average
42 or more	57 or more	High

Burnout Scale

On the burnout scale you will need to take an extra step. Starred items are "reverse scored." If you scored the item 1, write a 5 beside it. The reason we ask you to reverse the scores is because

You Wrote	Change to
	5
2	4
3	3
4	2
5	1

scientifically the measure works better when these questions are asked in a positive way

*1._____ = _____
*4._____ = _____
8._____
10._____
*15._____ = _____
*17._____ = _____
19._____
21._____
26._____
*29._____ = _____

Total:_____

The sum of my Burnout Questions is	So My Score Equals	And my Burnout level is
22 or less	43 or less	Low
Between 23 and 41	Around 50	Average
42 or more	57 or more	High

though they can tell us more about their negative form. For example, question 1. "I am happy" tells us more about the effects of helping when you are *not* happy so you reverse the score.

Secondary Traumatic Stress Scale

Just like you did on Compassion Satisfaction, copy your rating on each of these questions on to this table and add them up. When you have added then up you can find your score on the table to the right.

2_____
5_____
7_____
9_____
11_____
13_____
14_____
23_____
25_____
28_____

Total:_____

The sum of my Secondary Trauma Questions is	So My Score Equals	And my Secondary Traumatic Stress level is
22 or less	43 or less	Low
Between 23 and 41	Around 50	Average
42 or more	57 or more	High

YOUR SCORES ON THE PROQOL: PROFESSIONAL QUALITY OF LIFE SCREENING

Based on your responses, place your personal scores below. If you have any concerns, you should discuss them with a physical or mental health care professional.

Compassion Satisfaction _____

Compassion satisfaction is about the pleasure you derive from being able to do your work well. For example, you may feel like it is a pleasure to help others through your work. You may feel positively about your colleagues or your ability to contribute to the work setting or even the greater good of society. Higher scores on this scale represent a greater satisfaction related to your ability to be an effective caregiver in your job.

The average score is 50 (SD 10: alpha scale reliability .88). About 25% of people score higher than 57 and about 25% of people score below 43. If you are in the higher range, you probably derive a good deal of professional satisfaction from your position. If your scores are below 40, you may either find problems with your job, or there may be some other reason—for example, you might derive your satisfaction from activities other than your job.

Burnout _____

Most people have an intuitive idea of what burnout is. From the research perspective, burnout is one of the elements of Compassion Fatigue (CF) It is associated with feelings of hopelessness and difficulties in dealing with work or in doing your job effectively. These negative feelings usually have a gradual onset. They can reflect the feeling that your efforts make no difference, or they can be associated with a very high workload or a non-supportive work environment Higher scores on this scale mean that you are at higher risk for burnout.

The average score on the burnout scale is 50 (SD 10: alpha scale reliability .75). About 25% of people score above 57 and about 25% of people score below 43. If your score is below 43, this probably reflects positive feelings about your ability to be effective in your work. If you score above 57 you may wish to think about what at work makes you feel like you are not effective in your position. Your score may reflect your mood; perhaps you were having a "bad day" or are in need of some time off. If the high score persists or if it is reflective of other worries, it may be a cause for concern.

Secondary Traumatic Stress _____

The second component of Compassion Fatigue (CF) is secondary traumatic stress (STS). It is about your work related, secondary exposure to extremely or traumatically stressful events. Developing problems due to exposure to other's trauma is somewhat rare but does happen to many people who care for those who have experienced extremely or traumatically stressful events. For example, you may repeatedly near stories about the traumatic things that happen to other people commonly called Vicarious Traumatization. If your work puts you directly m the path of danger, for example. field work in a war or area of civil violence, this is not secondary exposure; your exposure is primary. However, if you are exposed to others' traumatic events as a result of your work, for example, as a therapist or an emergency worker, this is secondary exposure. The symptoms of STS are usually rapid in onset and associated with a particular event. They may include being afraid, having difficulty sleeping, having images of the upsetting event pop into your mind, or avoiding things that remind you of the event.

The average score on this scale is 50 (SD 10: alpha scale reliability. 81) About 25% of people score below 43 and about 25% of people score above 57. If your score is above 57, you may want to take some time to think about what at work may be frightening to you or if there is some other reason for the elevated score. While higher scores do not mean that you do have a problem, they are an indication that you may want to examine how you feel about your work and your work environment. You may wish to discuss this with your supervisor, a colleague, or a health care professional.

SELF-ASSESSMENT USING THE SKOVHOLT PRACTITIONER PROFESSIONAL RESILIENCY AND SELF-CARE INVENTORY

In addtion to the ProQOL, the Skovholt Practitioner Professional Resilience and Self-Care Inventory (Skorholt and Trotter-Matheson, 2011) can be used to assess how you are doing with self-care and resilience. This is relevant for professionals in all disciplines and has been widely used. It may be helpful to complete both the ProQOL and the Skovholt instrument to get a comprehensive look at how you are doing in the following areas:

- Professional vitality
- Personal vitality
- Professional stress
- Personal stress

CHECKLIST

SKOVHOLT PRACTITIONER PROFESSIONAL RESILIENCY AND SELF-CARE INVENTORY

The purpose of the inventory is to provide self-reflection for practitioners and students in the helping, health, and caring professions, broadly defined. All of these fields are relationship-intense fields where the welfare of the other (client, patient, student, advisee, mentee etc.) is primary. "Practitioner" here refers to individuals in these professions. All of these professions are distinct, with specialized areas of knowledge and techniques. However, they are united by the enormous amount of emotional investment needed for the I-Thou relationship with the other who is often experiencing a kind of suffering or human need of one kind or another.

Questions are addressed both to active practitioners and also to students in training programs across the broad range of the caring / relationship-intense professions. Some of the questions are more relevant to some professionals or students in some training programs than others.

The checklist consists of four sub-scales: Professional Vitality, Personal Vitality, Professional Stress and Personal Stress.

Circle your Responses:
1=Strongly Disagree, **2**=Disagree, **3**=Undecided, **4**=Agree, **5**=Strongly Agree

Professional Vitality

1. I find my work as a practitioner or as a student to be meaningful. 1 2 3 4 5
2. I view self-care as an ongoing part of my professional work/student life 1 2 3 4 5
3. I am interested in making positive attachments with my clients/students/patients. 1 2 3 4 5
4. I have the energy to make these positive attachments with my clients/students/patients 1 2 3 4 5
5. The director/chair at my site/school is dedicated to practitioner welfare 1 2 3 4 5
6. On the dimension of control of my work/schooling, I am closer to high control
   than low control. 1 2 3 4 5
7. On the dimension of demands at my work/schooling, I have reasonable demands rather
   than excessive demands from others 1 2 3 4 5
8. My work environment is like a greenhouse where everything grows, because the conditions
   are such that I feel supported in my professional work 1 2 3 4 5

Subscale Score for Professional Vitality (Possible score is 8-40) _____

Personal Vitality

9. I have plenty of humor and laughter in my life. 1 2 3 4 5
10. I have a strong code of values/ethics that gives me a sense of direction and integrity. 1 2 3 4 5
11. I feel loved by intimate others. 1 2 3 4 5
12. I have positive/close friendships 1 2 3 4 5
13. I am physically active and receive the benefits of exercise 1 2 3 4 5
14. My financial life (expenses, savings and spending) is in balance 1 2 3 4 5
15. I have a lot of fun in my life. 1 2 3 4 5
16. I have one or more abundant sources of high energy for my life
    (friends and family, pleasurable hobby, enjoyable pet, the natural world, a favorite activity) 1 2 3 4 5
17. To balance the ambiguity of work in the caring professions, I have some concrete activities that I
    enjoy where results are clear-cut (a collection such as coins / rocks / dolls, gardening, a fantasy sports
    team, weaving, remodeling and painting, fixing up a car) 1 2 3 4 5

18. My eating habits are good for my body 1 2 3 4 5
19. My sleep pattern is restorative. 1 2 3 4 5

Subscale Score for Personal Vitality (Possible score is 11-55) _____

Professional Stress

20. There are many contradictory messages about both practicing self-care and
    meeting expectations of being a highly competent practitioner / student. I am
    working to find a way through these contradictory messages. 1 2 3 4 5
21. Overall, I have been able to find a satisfactory level of "boundaried generosity"
    (defined as having both limits and giving of oneself) in my work with clients/students/patients. . . . 1 2 3 4 5
22. Witnessing human suffering is central in the caring professions (for example, client grief,
    student failure, patient physical pain). I am able to be very present to this suffering, but not be
    overwhelmed by it or experience too much of what is called "sadness of the soul" 1 2 3 4 5
23. I have found a way to have high standards for my work yet avoid unreachable perfectionism 1 2 3 4 5
24. My work is intrinsically pleasurable most of the time 1 2 3 4 5
25. Although judging success in the caring professions is often confusing, I have been able to
    find useful ways to judge my own professional success 1 2 3 4 5
26. I have at least one very positive relationship with a clinical supervisor / mentor / teacher 1 2 3 4 5
27. I am excited to learn new ideas/methods/theories/techniques in my field 1 2 3 4 5
28. The level of conflict between staff / faculty at my organization is low 1 2 3 4 5

Subscale Score for Professional Stress (Possible score is 9-45) _____

Personal Stress

29. There are different ways that I can get away from stress and relax (TV and videos, meditating,
    reading, social media, watching sports) 1 2 3 4 5
30. My personal life does not have an excessive number of one-way caring relationships where
    I am the caring one 1 2 3 4 5
31. My level of physical pain / disability is tolerable 1 2 3 4 5
32. My family relations are satisfying 1 2 3 4 5
33. I derive strength from my personal values and /or spiritual, religious practices and beliefs 1 2 3 4 5
34. I am not facing major betrayal in my personal life 1 2 3 4 5
35. I have one or more supportive communities where I feel connected 1 2 3 4 5
36. I am able to cope with significant losses in my life 1 2 3 4 5
37. I have time for reflective activities (alone: journaling, expressive writing, solitude or, with
    others: talking through concerns with others) 1 2 3 4 5
38. When I feel the need, I am able to get help for myself 1 2 3 4 5

Subscale Score for Personal Stress (Possible score is 10-50) _____
Total Score for the Four Subscales (Possible score is 38-190) _____

There is a total of 38 questions in the Skovholt Professional Resiliency and Self-Care Inventory. All are scored in a positive direction with from 0 (low) to 5 (high). As stated earlier, the scoring system is a method for self-reflection by practitioners and students in the caring professions. There is no total number that is considered best.

As a way to consider professional resiliency and self-care in your career work, consider these questions:
First, scan the questions and focus on your high answers—those with 4 and 5 responses. What do you conclude?

_____

_____

_____

_____

Then focus on your low answers—those with 1and 2 responses. What do you conclude?

_____

_____

_____

_____

Then look across the four categories of Professional Vitality, Personal Vitality, Professional Stress and Personal Stress. Are they in balance? If not in balance, what remedies could you consider?

_____

_____

_____

_____

Copyright © 2010 Thomas M. Skovholt, 2014 Revised

RECOGNIZING EARLY WARNING SIGNALS

It is important to detect early warning signals of stress or distress before they become severe and impairing. This could be likened to paying attention to the yellow gas light on one's dashboard, which, if ignored, can lead to serious consequences. Therapists may not always be the best at detecting subtle distress reactions in themselves, which can be a prequel to more serious problems.

A helpful exercise is for therapists to periodically review the following list, referred to in an earlier section, to determine if any of these tell-tale signs are evident:

- frequently feeling tired
- arguing with others over minor things
- never being able to relax
- constantly feeling in demand or under pressure
- lack of patience or tolerance
- feeling there is not enough time for yourself, family or friends
- memory and concentration lapses
- lack of interest in or time to socialize or engage in recreational activities
- feeling irritable, tired and unfulfilled at the end of the work day

In addition, the following exercise can be helpful. Completing the form on the next page will help the therapist to identify characteristic stress markers, which can then be regularly monitored to allow early intervention.

EXERCISE

IDENTIFYING YOUR PERSONAL INDICATORS OF DISTRESS

Specify changes you notice during periods of stress in the following areas:

1. Changes in my behavior (irritability, withdrawal from others, lack of productivity)
   Specify:
   _____
   _____
   _____
   _____

2. Changes in my body (sleep problems, eating disturbances, headaches, tiredness)
   Specify:
   _____
   _____
   _____
   _____

3. Changes in my thinking (poor concentration, indecisiveness, pessimism, self-blame)
   Specify:
   _____
   _____
   _____
   _____

4. Changes that other people who know me have commented on or brought to my attention
   (friends or family say that I am snappy or that I have become distant or withdrawn)
   Specify:
   _____
   _____
   _____
   _____

IDENTIFYING CHARACTERISTIC STRESSORS

It can also be very helpful to identify relevant situational triggers or "stress buttons" which are likely to occur in your work situation. These will usually be specific to you and, in all probability, are likely to be influenced by personal characteristics, belief systems and expectations.

Identifying high-risk situations for lapse/relapse or the emergence of problems has considerable therapeutic benefit for a wide range of clients, as it allows planning and preparing in advance for these challenges. Likewise, you can learn to identify clinical or non-clinical situations in your own practice which can elicit certain stress reactions. This will be enormously helpful in taking steps to combat and deal with these trigger events more effectively.

Using the worksheet, identify situations which have the potential to elicit distress in you.

IDENTIFYING YOUR SOURCES OF STRESS

What are some stressors or triggers for distress for you in the work situation?

Client-Related Stressors/Triggers
Specify: _____

_____

_____

_____

_____

Administrative or Organizational Stressors/Triggers
Specify: _____

_____

_____

_____

_____

Other Stressors or Triggers
Specify: _____

_____

_____

_____

_____

HOW MANY BURNOUT/STRESS FACTORS DO YOU HAVE?

Maslach & Leiter (2008) have identified 7 key areas contributing to burnout and stress. Take a moment to honestly answer these questions to assess your own level of stress.

Do you:

Feel you have a sustainable workload? _____

Feel overloaded with work? _____

Do you:

Have a feeling of choice or control in your work environment? _____

Experience little or no control? _____

Do you:

Have a sense of reward and recognition at work? _____

Feel little or no recognition or reward? _____

Do you:

Experience a sense of community or belonging in your work environment? _____

See a breakdown in a sense of community or belonging? _____

Do you:

Experience fairness, justice and respect at work? _____

See little respect or fairness in your work setting? _____

Do you:

See your work as meaningful and in line with your values? _____

Experience a significant clash in values between you and the agency? _____

Do you:

See a good fit between you (who you are as a person) and your job? _____

Experience some disconnect between you (who you are as a person) and your job?

_____

If you answered most of the above items in the negative, you may struggle with significant external stress which needs to be dealt with by either a change in thinking or in the situation or both. Possible interventions will be discussed in the next section of this book.

The previous exercise may have helped you identify which stress factors are present in your work situation and to what extent these are creating problems. Another index of the intensity or impact of stressors is the following analysis. If we examine the dimensions of control, demand and support, it appears from the research that minimum job stress occurs when there is high control, low demand and high support. These three factors probably interact in a critical way and may exacerbate or diminish the effects of each other. For example, if an individual works in a highly stressful job where he has many demands made on him by clients and staff, the effects of this stressor (high demand) may be mitigated by the fact that the individual also feels he has a lot of support from his agency and perceives that he has some control over the environment (chooses to see challenging cases or opts for a high case load).If the same situation occurs (high demand from clients and staff) but is combined with a low level of support (or perceived support) from supervisors and staff plus a perceived lack of control of autonomy over the situation (more and more clients are scheduled without consultation or discussion) the individual is likely to be maximally stressed and potentially a candidate for burnout.

The worksheet on the following page will help to identify each of these factors (demand, control and support) in your work environment.

HOW MUCH CONTROL, DEMAND AND SUPPORT IS PRESENT IN YOUR SITUATION?

Establishing where you are on each of these three dimensions can be evaluated by asking yourself the following questions:

Control:

Do I feel I have influence over what happens at work?   Yes _____   No _____

Do I feel I have freedom to decide how I do my work?   Yes _____   No _____

Answering yes to both questions indicates high control, answering no to both indicates low control.

Demand:

Do I have to work very hard?   Yes _____   No _____

Do I not have enough time to get my work done?   Yes _____   No _____

Is my work load excessive?   Yes _____   No _____

Answering all three questions yes indicates high demand, answering all three no indicates low demand.

Support:

Do I work with helpful people who have an interest in me?   Yes _____   No _____

Do I have a supervisor who is helpful and who takes an interest in me?   Yes _____   No _____

Answering yes to both questions indicates high support, answering no to both indicates low support.

So, looking at the above and where you put yourself in terms of your work experience with control (high or low), demand (high or low), and support (high or low), might alert you to steps which may need to be taken to promote a greater sense of control, a reduced sense of demand, and an increased sense of support.

Stress is a combination of external and internal factors. That is to say we experience external stressors (client or organizational demands) which can be exacerbated by our own tendencies and predispositions which result in a consequent high level of distress or impairment. This, as readers will note, is consistent with the cognitive behavioral model described earlier in the text. This suggests that situations or external events do not lead directly to emotional or behavioral consequences but are mediated through thoughts and beliefs. This is often described as the ABC model where A= activating events, B= beliefs and C= consequences. While many people adopt an AC model where events lead straight to emotions ("He made me so mad when he said that"), it is clear that the ABC model is more accurate ("After he said that I got upset because that showed he has no respect for me"). Clearly beliefs and thoughts play a crucial role in stress reactions. In a work situation, for example, when a client consistently fails to follow through on homework assignments, this situation will trigger much greater distress in the therapist if she thinks, "He is doing this to interfere with my therapy," than if she thinks, "We need to work out what the obstacles to him doing homework are and find a way around these."

The exercise on the next page encourages you to identify external (situations) and internal (beliefs, behaviors and circumstances related to you) stressors which may both be involved in your stress reactions.

EXERCISE

IDENTIFYING YOUR EXTERNAL AND INTERNAL STRESSORS

The following checklist may be helpful in identifying both external and internal stressors.

External stressors

Do you experience the following?

_____ Low peer support

_____ Low supervisor support

_____ Insufficient salary or other rewards

_____ Many demanding clients

_____ Long hours

_____ No or poor on-job training

_____ High organizational conflict

_____ Little focus on personal development or self-care in agency

Internal stressors

Do you have problems with any of these?

_____ Poor professional boundaries

_____ Poor self-care

_____ Overly idealistic or unrealistic expectations of clients or agency

_____ Imbalanced lifestyle (lack of recreation)

_____ Intolerance of things not going well or of being unsuccessful

_____ Poor understanding of, or attending to, one's own needs

_____ Lack of a sustaining personal or spiritual life

_____ Perfectionism

_____ Inability to say "no"

_____ Lack of a sense of humor or being overly serious

_____ Perception of lack of success with clients

_____ Unfavorable comparisons (made by self) with colleagues

_____ Negative self-evaluation

_____ Failure to ask supervisors or peers for help

While it is obvious that the second group of stressors revolves around personal characteristics or beliefs, it is important to see that one's own perception may also influence the impact of the first group of stressors. For example, the experience of low supervisor support may be the reality, or alternately it may possibly be a misperception of the supervisor, or due to your not asking for help or support and presenting an image of "having everything together."

SPECIFIC NEGATIVE THOUGHTS AND GENERAL BELIEFS

This section deals with (1) specific negative thoughts which are moment-to-moment thoughts, images and memories which pass through our minds, usually in response to specific situations or when recalling things that happened or imagining things which could happen and (2) general beliefs which are assumptions or rules which underlie the negative thoughts and are not situation-specific but more general.

EXERCISE

IDENTIFYING YOUR NEGATIVE THOUGHTS

Do you find yourself thinking (indicate 4= Often, 3= Sometimes, 2 = Rarely or 1= Never)?

Regarding clients:

_____ There is no progress

_____ I am not helping this client at all

_____ If the client is angry or critical, I am not handling things properly

_____ He or she is resisting me and doesn't want to change or improve

_____ This person's situation is so realistically terrible that there is nothing I can do to help

_____ I get all the difficult cases like this one

Regarding work:

_____ My supervisor or colleagues are totally unsupportive of me

_____ I will never get this paperwork done

_____ Everybody is dumping on me

_____ Why do I bother when I get so few rewards, financial or otherwise?

IDENTIFYING YOUR DYSFUNCTIONAL BELIEFS

This refers to general assumptions, rules or beliefs, which individuals adopt and which profoundly influence how experiences are viewed and interpreted.

Do you believe (indicate 3= Strongly, 2 = Somewhat sometimes, 1= Not at all)?

Regarding clients:

_____ I have to be successful with all my clients all the time

_____ I must always have good sessions with my clients

_____ I should not dislike any of my clients

_____ I should not feel any negative emotions related to clients or to doing therapy with them

_____ My clients should always respect and like me

_____ People I am trying to help should not be difficult and resistant

_____ If I extend myself to help clients, they ought to be motivated to change and reward me for my efforts

Regarding your work and yourself:

_____ I must always be totally competent and in control

_____ It is terrible to be criticized or disapproved of

_____ Life in the workplace should be fair and just

_____ My worth as a person is dependent on my job performance

_____ If I am not successful in alleviating clients' problems, I can't feel good about myself

_____ I must always have good judgment as a professional

_____ I should have all the answers

_____ I should not have any strong emotional reactions myself

_____ If I have emotional or other problems, I should control them and never show them to clients or colleagues

_____ I should not seek help from peers, supervisors or professionally

_____ I will be seen as weak if I ask for help

_____ I must have things the way I want them

_____ Other people should see things my way

_____ I must be perceived as totally competent

RECOGNIZING THINKING PATTERNS THAT CAN LEAD TO DISTRESS

Identifying dysfunctional thinking

The steps outlined in the next section to identify negative thoughts and beliefs will be familiar to counselors who use cognitive behavior therapy in their practice. However, many mental health or health care providers in general may not have used these methods to carefully examine their own emotional reactions when engaged in their work. This systematic approach can be easily and effectively implemented in episodes of distress or emotional upset at work by asking oneself the following questions:

1. Is there a noticeable shift in feelings experienced (an onset of distress or upset)?
2. What are the specific emotions experienced and what is the intensity of each on a 0-100 scale?
3. What is the situation eliciting the distressing emotions (the trigger event)?
4. What are the relevant thoughts and beliefs about this situation which influence the emotions or feelings experienced?

It should be possible to dismantle an episode of distress and identify:

- An emotion (anger, irritation, sadness, anxiety) and its intensity (0-100)
- A trigger situation (client behavior, therapy impasse, non-client related problem)
- Thoughts which follow from the trigger and lead to the emotion

Automatic thoughts linking the situation and the emotion

For example, imagine the following scenario:

You notice that during a session your emotional state has changed (Question 1) and you are becoming anxious (Question 2). This emotion has an intensity of 70 on a 0-100 scale (Question 2). You started to become anxious as the client began talking about how frustrated he feels that he is no better after seeing you for 6 weeks (Question 3). You catch yourself thinking, " What if he drops out of therapy or what if he is so demoralized that he becomes actively suicidal?"(Question 4).

This is a clear example of the CBT model with a situation (the client stating that he is frustrated), leading to specific automatic thoughts ("What if he drops out of therapy or becomes actively suicidal?"), leading to emotions (anxiety). Having established this connection, the next step is to test and challenge the identified thoughts. It may be helpful to practice this step (identifying the situation-thoughts-feelings link) by imagining the following scenarios:

Situation 1: Despite your best efforts, a client gives you the following feedback: "You don't really seem to care what happens to me. You don't have any problems so you can't understand what I am going through. I am just a way that you make a living and am not of any importance to you."

How might you feel?_____

_____

What emotions might be triggered by this? _____

_____

_____

What thoughts might you have concerning what the client said?

_____

_____

What meaning might this have for you?

_____

_____

Situation 2: You have just heard from the hospital admissions department that a client you see, who has been doing well, has had a relapse, is severely depressed and is being hospitalized with suicidal ideation.

How might you feel?

_____

_____

What emotions might be triggered by this?

_____

_____

What thoughts might you have concerning this?

_____

_____

What meaning might this have for you?

_____

_____

Situation 3: You have a full caseload and are feeling pressured and stressed. Your agency director tells you that, due to cutbacks, you will have to see some extra clients one evening a week.

How might you feel?

_____

_____

What emotions might be triggered by this?

_____

_____

What thoughts might you have?

_____

_____

What meaning might this have for you?

_____

_____

In the above examples when you put yourself in these situations and imagine your reactions, do you begin to see how situations, thoughts and feelings interact? The mediating role that certain thoughts play in creating negative feelings may also be clearly seen.

Retrospective analysis

Another useful thought identification method is for a caregiver to retrospectively focus on a recent time doing therapy when feelings of frustration, anxiety or irritation occurred. For example, recall an episode where you experienced some level of distress due to a client. Identifying the situation and emotion can be facilitated by asking the questions listed below:

- What was the situation?
- What happened?
- What feelings did I have?
- What thoughts did I have?
- What was going through my mind when I began to feel upset in this situation?
- What meaning did it have for me?
- Why was it a problem?

The three-column form on the next page provides a useful way of identifying the components of an episode of workplace distress by allowing us to systematically examine the different components of the problem, including the situation, associated thoughts and subsequent feelings. With this information we can then proceed to thought challenging or other self-directed interventions which will be described later.

IDENTIFYING THE SITUATION, FEELINGS AND THOUGHTS

This form is intended to help you identify specific negative thoughts at times of upset and connect these with the trigger situation and specific emotions you experience. When you are upset or as soon after as you can, fill out the following 3 columns going from left to right.

Feelings	Situation	Thoughts
Rate intensity. What was I feeling? How bad was the feeling? (0-100)	Where was I? What was going on?	What went through my mind? What did it mean to me?

Chapter 5
Intervention

To return to the road journey metaphor, we ideally want to be able to fix any problems which come up which are impeding us on our journey (get the flat tire fixed, get back on the right road). Likewise, if we are struggling with some of the issues mentioned in this book we would clearly want to put things right or at least intervene so that our level of distress is reduced.

However, before moving to specific intervention strategies, we would reiterate that accurate recognition of a problem always precedes finding an effective solution. When working with clients, we often struggle to provide help to them when the nature of the problem is unclear or not articulated. Similarly, without the insight or knowledge on our part that something is wrong, there is no motivation for us to change and no likelihood that actual change will occur since no interventions strategies will be initiated.

Another reason we include detection as an integral first stage in the process of intervention is that "a stitch in time saves nine." The earlier the recognition of a problem the greater the chance of a speedy and effective solution. The driver who ignores the fuel light on his or her dashboard runs the risk of running out of gas and having a major problem later in contrast to the immediate and minor issue of stopping at a gas station when it comes on.

For all of these reasons we will return briefly to the recognition of warning signals, which was described in the Detection section, before proceeding to describe powerful intervention methods for dealing with the issues of compassion fatigue, stress and burnout.

CHECKLIST

ARE THE SIGNS AND SYMPTOMS BUILDING UP?

If you're concerned that you may be developing caregiver stress, it may be helpful to take the time to consider whether you have the signs and symptoms. Take a moment to reflect on your own observations and the feedback you may be getting from other people.

Physical signs:

_____ I am sore and tired at the end of a day at work

_____ I am getting sick more often, I feel like my health is getting worse

_____ I'm noticing changes in my energy level

_____ When I wake up in the morning I'm still tired

_____ I get tired more easily and don't feel rested very often

Behavioral changes:

_____ Sometimes people ask me if I'm okay, saying that I seem irritable or tired

_____ I am more short-tempered and impatient than I used to be

_____ I don't think as quickly or creatively as I used to

_____ I am not as patient as I used to be

_____ Sometimes I have a hard time enjoying tender, intimate feelings

Emotional impact:

_____ My sense of humor is off; I'm more cynical and sarcastic

_____ People annoy me more easily

_____ My level of empathy is lower than usual

_____ There are times I just want to be left alone

_____ I'm preoccupied with the suffering of others

Work-related symptoms

_____ My boundaries are less clear, either too loose or too rigid

_____ I don't feel appreciated by my employer

_____ I work with an unusually stressful population

_____ Sometimes I don't feel like I am able to help enough

_____ My work life and personal life tend to bleed together

HOW ARE YOU DOING WITH SELF-CARE?

So many people with caregiver stress don't take very good care of themselves. Over time, healthy habits and solid self-care practice may go by the wayside. If you are feeling that you may be experiencing symptoms of caregiver stress, take a look at this checklist to size up how well you are doing with your self-care practices.

_____ I am exercising regularly

_____ My drinking or drug use is reasonable and not a problem

_____ I continue to participate in pleasurable activities or hobbies

_____ I enjoy being outside or seeing natural beauty

_____ My social life is satisfying

_____ Friends and family seem to enjoy being around me

_____ I am getting regular health care

_____ I sleep well

_____ My eating habits are healthy

_____ I can relax

_____ I take time off work on a regular basis

_____ I feel that I'm productive at work

_____ My boundaries at work remain clear

_____ I feel supported by my employer

_____ My colleagues and I work well together

_____ I am paid adequately

_____ I laugh easily

_____ I have spiritual beliefs that are important to me

_____ I have something to offer at work

_____ I have a full life outside of work

MOTIVATION FOR CHANGE

Having detected some issues that need to be addressed regarding work stress, the next step is to review our own motivation to make the changes required. One useful way to assess motivation and willingness to change is by using the following transtheoretical model of change first proposed by Prochaska and DiClemente (1984) and often used in addiction treatment. Their hypothesis was that change occurs in a series of stages. These stages are:

> It's quite clear that once you've started to show signs of caregiver stress it's important to intervene quickly. By the time it becomes evident that a problem is developing it's time to take action.

Pre-Contemplation: when the individual is unsure or ambivalent about whether change is necessary

Contemplation: when the individual thinks that he or she may need to change

Preparation: when the individual knows he or she needs to change and is considering how to make this happen

Action: when the individual is beginning to initiate these changes

Maintenance: when the individual is maintaining the changes and not backsliding

It is important for any of us who are thinking about changing any habits (in this case, poor self-care habits) to honestly assess where we are in this process and attempt to move through the stages. So we would suggest, after identifying your stress level or quality of functioning in the previous section that you complete the form on the next page.

DO YOU REALLY WANT TO CHANGE?

When you think about your work-related stress (such as a problem you need to manage better), it will be helpful to indicate **honestly** which of these statements best describes where you are now. Put a check next to one or more which best fits your current situation.

_____ I may not need to make changes (Pre Contemplation)

_____ Maybe I need to change (Contemplation)

_____ I am considering how to change (Preparation)

_____ I am starting to make changes (Action)

_____ I am maintaining these changes (Maintenance)

Ideally, to get the most from this workbook you would be at the Preparation, Action or Maintenance stage, but if you are at the Pre-contemplation or Contemplation stage you can also benefit. If this is the case, we would suggest that a way to increase motivation for change would be to carry out a costs-benefits or pros and cons analysis, as will be described below and in the next exercise.

Many of our clients can be ambivalent about change in that they feel they probably should change some aspects of their lives or behavior but they are also unsure if they can change or if change will be worth the effort. Similarly, professional caregivers, who experience some of the difficulties with stress described in this workbook, may have mixed feelings about making some of the changes necessary to reduce stress or to take better care of themselves. On the one hand, they recognize that it is in their best interest to reduce high levels of stress, but on the other hand, they may consider the actual steps involved in effecting change (saying "no" to unreasonable requests, exercising regularly, seeking peer support) too overwhelming or too difficult to carry out.

It is recommended that anyone contemplating changing existing habits or maintaining new habits carry out a detailed analysis of the advantages and disadvantages of change rather than just give 'lip service' to the idea of change. Only when the benefits of change are clearly seen to outweigh the costs associated with change or, alternatively, only when the costs of maintaining the current situation (making no change) are seen to outweigh the benefits of staying the same does "true" rather than "artificial" motivation emerge. To this end, the exercise on the next page will assist in this analysis and hopefully stimulate a genuine motivation to change.

EXERCISE

WHAT WILL BE THE BENEFITS AND COSTS OF CHANGING FOR YOU?

Whenever we are on the fence regarding whether we need to make changes or have difficulty seeing the payoff, it is worth considering what we gain or lose from both staying as we are and from making a change. So first, consider and write down what will happen if you carry on the way you are regarding self-care. Second, consider and write down what you think might happen if you did make some changes to ensure better self-care.

Costs of staying the same	Benefits of staying the same

Costs of changing	Benefits of changing

How does it look? Do you see some benefits in changing and some costs to staying the same?

_____

_____

_____

_____

EXERCISE

How Committed and Able Are You to Make Changes?

Are you ready to make changes? _____
_____
_____
_____

If so, what changes are you preparing to make?_____
_____
_____
_____

Do you feel confident you can change in these ways?_____
_____
_____
_____

If not, why not? _____
_____
_____
_____

If you doubt your ability to change, recall some things you have changed in your life up to now which were not easy but which you accomplished despite this (such as giving up smoking, sticking to a weight loss program or going back to college).

If you are ready to make a commitment to change, you might decide to commit privately (write it down here or elsewhere) or publicly (tell others what you intend to do). Either way, we suggest writing it down and displaying it somewhere where you will be reminded of this commitment regularly.

If you feel ready to be active in making this change, specify again in writing what you will do to make it happen. Later in the workbook there will be opportunities to come up with action plans in writing.

HIGH PRIORITY ON SELF-CARE

*"Too often, we therapists neglect our personal relationships. Our work
becomes our life. At the end of our workday, having given so much of ourselves,
we feel drained of desire for more relationship."*

—I.D. Yalom

*"Overall, we recommend that therapists do for themselves the self-nurturing, self-building things
they would have their clients do. Increasing our awareness of our needs and remaining connected
with our bodies, our feelings, and other people will strengthen us as individuals and allow
us to choose to continue to do this important work."*

—L.A. Pearlman

Several professional governing bodies stress the importance of managing potential impairment as part of their codes of ethics. The American Counseling Association's code of ethics (ACA 2014) states:

> Counselors monitor themselves for signs of impairment from their own physical, mental or emotional problems and refrain from offering or providing professional services when impaired. They seek assistance for problems that reach the level of professional impairment, and, if necessary, they limit, suspend, or terminate their professional responsibilities until it is determined that they may safely resume their work.

Marriage and family therapists are also bound by their ethical code (AAMFT 2012) as follows:

> Marriage and family therapists seek appropriate professional assistance for their personal problems or conflicts that may impair work performance or clinical judgment.

And, for one more example of an ethical mandate, we can look to the ethical code of the National Association of Social Workers (NASW 2008) which states:

Social workers whose personal problems, psychosocial distress, legal problems, substance abuse, or mental health difficulties interfere with their professional judgment and performance should immediately seek consultation and take appropriate remedial action by seeking professional help, making adjustments in workload, terminating practice, or taking any other steps necessary to protect clients and others.

Those are some pretty sobering and clear reminders to place a high priority on self-care and wellness. Pearlman and Maclan (1995) surveyed a group of trauma therapists to figure out what activities were most helpful in balancing out their trauma exposure. Here is a list of things that they found helpful, along with the percentage of therapists who reported benefit from the activity:

85% Discussed cases with colleagues

76% Attended workshops

70% Spent time with family and friends

70% Travel, vacation, hobbies, movies

69% Talked with colleagues between sessions

64% Socialized

62% Exercised

56% Limited caseload

44% Developed spiritual life

44% Received regular supervision

Lower on the list, but still noted as effective, were activities such as teaching, giving supervision, performing community service, receiving bodywork or massage, writing, journaling, engaging in social justice work, conducting research, referring out clients who might activate the therapist's issues, and engaging in supervision.

Based on the discussion so far we would now encourage you to think of some general strategies which might help you deal with workplace stress.

Action Plan for Distress Management

It is important to be active in making the changes required rather than just giving lip service to the idea that you need to change.

List below all the things you could do to deal with your distress. The list can include anything which reduced your distress in the past and any ideas that you have heard or read about (including in this book) which you think might be helpful.

1._____

_____

2._____

_____

3._____

_____

4._____

_____

5._____

_____

6._____

_____

7._____

_____

8._____

_____

9._____

_____

10._____

_____

11._____

_____

12._____

_____

With regard to more specific ways we could modify and reduce stress generated from our work as health care providers we could consider interventions in the following broad areas:

- Self-directed
- Peer or supervisor
- Organizational
- Professional

Self-directed

To return briefly to the road journey metaphor, in the event of our car running out of gas or developing a relatively minor problem, we can often by our own efforts get it running again. This is equivalent to a provider recognizing an ongoing problem as detailed earlier and without external assistance using personal strategies to deal with the issue.

DISTRESS REDUCTION IN THE WORKPLACE

A number of books offer suggestions on effectively dealing with stress in the workplace (Farber 1983; Klareich, 1990; Lederer & Hall, 1999; Koettler, 1999; Ludgate, 2012). These incorporate strategies and interventions based on cognitive behavioral and related approaches. In addition, we offer the following suggestions based on ideas presented at our seminars for those dealing with caregiver distress or burnout.

- Watch for early signs of distress and take action as soon as possible.
- Identify any external stressors. Reduce these sources of distress when possible or alternately develop effective coping skills when they cannot be reduced.
- In each of episode of distress consider the contribution made by: (a) the situation itself and, (b) the associated thoughts or thinking style in creating the distress reaction.
- Define concretely the problem(s) involved. Dismantle the problem into the components of situations, thoughts and feelings.
- Check out and deal with any dysfunctional cognitions identified.
- Become an effective problem solver by brainstorming all possible solutions, evaluating the pros and cons of each, selecting the most feasible, putting this into action and reviewing the results.
- Do not make self-esteem contingent on work or work performance.
- Keep things in perspective and avoid catastrophizing.
- Make sure not to personalize negative events.
- Do not engage in overgeneralization, black or white thinking or other cognitive distortions (these will be described later).
- Have realistic expectations and avoid the messiah complex. Do not assume that you can be superman or superwoman.
- Set realistic, achievable goals for yourself and monitor progress towards these. Give yourself credit for achieving these and recognize small gains in a positive direction.
- Examine the role of personal behavior in maintaining or creating distress. Identify anything you are doing which makes a bad situation worse.

- Plan to reduce or eliminate self-defeating behaviors from your repertoire. How adaptive are the coping strategies currently being used? Abandon any which create their own problems (such as drinking or overeating).

- Substitute healthy stress management techniques (meditation, yoga, relaxation techniques, exercise or visualization) for any unhealthy or destructive ones.

- Utilize a whole variety of "stress busters," which may potentially work based on past experience and current resources available.

- Give up trying to control the behavior of others; this is a set-up for frustration. It is important to realize that you can be an influence, but not exert control over other people including clients, colleagues, family and friends.

- Use humor and realize that events can always be seen from another (less serious) perspective. In particular, be willing and able to make fun of yourself (not your clients) and in the process create an alternative view of the situation.

- Develop a personalized emotional fire drill. Plan in advance strategies which can be implemented at times of acute distress.

- Take a more compassionate attitude toward yourself. Act as you would toward a beloved friend or family member, giving the same support and encouragement.

- Look after yourself better in terms of rest, diet and exercise.

General guidelines for providers who work with challenging cases

Before proceeding to detailed descriptions of specific cognitive behavioral interventions to deal with your emotional reactions, some general suggestions will be offered for working more effectively with challenging cases (this might include traumatized individuals, those with chronic problems, terminal illness and highly suicidal individuals) without setting yourself up for distress.

- Maintain a problem-solving attitude. Even when faced with obstacles, try to remain calm, collaboratively attempting to identify what is interfering with progress, generating alternative solutions and adopting a plan.

- When an impasse occurs, do not attribute responsibility for this to either the client or yourself, but see it as a problem to be solved and attempt to generate possible solutions.

- Avoid labeling or stereotyping the client. Instead try to use the client case formulation (how you conceptualize the client and his or her issues) to understand what is going on for this person in this present situation. For example, how does what seems like "resistance" fit in with the client's beliefs and individual history? It may be that the person values being in control.

- Identify and deal with your own dysfunctional cognitions.

- Be realistic in your expectations. Avoid the trap of thinking that no one will ever relapse, have setbacks or not show a good response to the application of techniques which usually prove helpful to other clients. In addition, do not expect linear progress. It is more likely to be in a somewhat zigzag fashion with stops and starts, even when the client is improving.

- Try to remain guardedly optimistic. Therapist hopelessness, cynicism or pessimism will interfere with therapeutic progress just as these attitudes in the client can. The provider should promote the idea that some change in some facets of the client's functioning is always possible and communicate this to the client without creating false or irrational expectations.

- Maintain a high level of tolerance for frustration. Professionals working with challenging cases should expect, and be prepared for, roadblocks and frustration. A comprehensive case formulation should allow a prediction of what difficulties are likely to come up in treatment itself or in the therapy relationship, based on the client's beliefs and compensatory strategies, arising in part out of previous learning experiences. Being forewarned in this way, the provider may be able to plan in advance for these problems and adapt the delivery of therapy accordingly.

- Avoid buying into the client's distortions. Even when an individual's situation is realistically "bad," it is important, while acknowledging this reality, to also examine the possible influence of negative thinking or inadequate coping in "making a bad situation worse."

- Resist the urge to switch models or approaches inconsistently when the going gets tough. It is possible to creatively interweave therapeutic interventions from other models or approaches, while still being guided by the original model. The unsystematic application of many techniques or models is likely to be ineffective, and possibly confusing and anti-therapeutic, for the client.

- Do not expect or believe that you will have all the answers to every problem. It sometimes goes against the grain for some providers, who have unrealistic expectations for themselves, to say to a client, "I am not sure what the answer is, but I will try and find out by consulting with colleagues or the literature." But, in fact, this may model for the client effective problem-solving without expectations of being perfect or all-competent.

USING CBT TO REDUCE DISTRESS AND BURNOUT

Cognitive behavioral strategies which providers can use as self-therapy have been described by several writers in the field. J.S. Beck (2005) describes a method of carrying out emotional self-scanning when working with challenging cases. By such means, therapists and other providers can develop skills in detecting a change in their thinking, emotions, behavior, or physiology, which can cue them to the presence of a relational or other problem. For example, what thoughts and feelings emerge when you review your schedule for the day? Feelings of discomfort in anticipation of seeing someone, or hoping that a particular client may cancel, are an index of some negative feelings and associated distressing thoughts about specific clients. Beck demonstrates how to modify these feelings and thoughts by questioning their validity, looking for distortions in thinking and using other cognitive techniques. Practically speaking, providers working with challenging cases might identify their emotional reactions on an ongoing basis or as needed by asking themselves questions such as:

- Am I feeling any negative reactions, such as anger, irritation, hopelessness or anxiety?

- Am I engaging in any dysfunctional behaviors, such as blaming, demeaning or controlling my client?

- What predictions am I making concerning how this person will behave in today's session?

If your answers to these questions reveal problems, then you might need to intervene to reduce your distress and increase effectiveness with the client, as this will in all probability be diminished by having such reactions. Similarly, Leahy (1996) suggests that providers pay close attention to distortions which may arise in their thinking about themselves or their patients. For example, recognizing that the thought, "last week's progress with this client was just an illusion" is an example of a particular cognitive distortion (disqualifying the positive) will lead to more balanced, adaptive and functional thinking concerning the therapeutic issues with a client whose progress is fluctuating. Layden et al. (1993) describe the steps a therapist working with clients diagnosed with borderline personality disorder could take to alleviate their own dysfunctional thoughts and feelings of distress which are often triggered by issues arising in treating these individuals.

CBT writers have also stressed the importance of therapists establishing more functional belief systems (which foster a coping or problem-solving set) rather than a blaming attitude (which involves scapegoating either oneself or the client for the problems experienced in therapy). Lastly, it has been suggested that limited self-disclosure, where the provider shares some of his or her feelings of frustration or anxiety, may be therapeutic for both the caregiver and the client, provided this is done carefully and with consideration of the possible consequences.

Historically, cognitive behavioral therapists have tended to avoid terms like transference and countertransference, as these terms are associated with the psychoanalytic tradition. However, in dealing with complex and challenging cases, client-therapist relationship factors are more important than in more standard applications of CBT. When working with personality-disordered clients this may, of necessity, become a major therapeutic focus (Beck et al, 2005; Layden, Newman, Freeman & Morse, 1993). The therapist may need to look for schemas and belief systems, possibly acquired in childhood or early experiences, which are being activated by the therapy relationship. This can help explain many therapy-interfering behaviors on the part of the client and can also prevent frustration with the client building up. Leahy (1996) also suggests that it is important for therapists to understand how their own schemas and belief systems may create certain vulnerabilities and make it more likely that they will be upset by certain situations, which are logically linked to this vulnerability. It can be instructive for therapists to ask themselves questions such as:

- Which kind of clients or client situations tend to create strong feelings in me?
- Which kinds of problems in therapy lead to non-therapeutic behaviors on my part?
- Which clients feel like friends and are hard to confront?

Having identified some of these "hot spots," the next step is to try to determine the core beliefs or schemas that are activated by these situations and where they came from. Another way of identifying these beliefs, Leahy suggests, is by the therapist asking him or herself:

- What is my worst fear concerning a negative outcome in therapy (being sued, failing, or being attacked)?
- If this did happen, what would it mean about me? (I am a failure, I am vulnerable.)
- How do the client's situation and my beliefs and behaviors fit together? (If the client acts out, I should not confront him, as he may leave therapy and I will then have failed.)

The idea of providers using the same techniques with themselves that are effective in reducing distress in clients is not new. More than 30 years ago, Albert Ellis (Ellis, 1983), one of the pioneers in the evolution of CBT, described some general principles for dealing with emotional disturbance arising out doing the work of a therapist. He encouraged therapists to:

- Identify irrational beliefs underlying therapeutic upsets, especially those involving absolutistic thinking ("I should be able to help everyone I see").
- Consider these as hypotheses to be tested and challenged.
- Review disconfirming evidence.
- Create alternative, rational, preferential statements ("I would like to help all my clients").
- Make sure that self-acceptance is not conditional on therapeutic success or being liked by clients.
- Refuse to "awfulize" about things which are challenging (a client not doing their homework is annoying or inconvenient rather than terrible).
- Persistently act against these irrational beliefs (show yourself that, in fact, obnoxious behavior can actually be tolerated).

> Are we alone, however, in our belief that we, as care givers, don't do such a good job in applying these CBT tools, of known effectiveness, to ourselves?

Before moving to self-directed CBT intervention, a CBT conceptualization can greatly aid in understanding caregiver distress. We might think about a particular episode of work-related distress following the model we outlined previously.

IDENTIFYING THE SITUATION, FEELINGS AND THOUGHTS

Ask yourself the following questions:

- Is there a noticeable shift in feelings experienced (an onset of distress or upset)?
- What are the specific emotions experienced and what is the intensity of each on a 0-100 scale?
- What is the situation eliciting the distressing emotions (the trigger event)?
- What are the relevant thoughts and beliefs about this situation which influence the emotions or feelings experienced?

At this point you should be able to identify examples of:

- An emotion (anger, irritation, sadness, anxiety) and its intensity (0-100)
- A trigger situation (client behavior, therapy impasse, not a client-related problem)
- Automatic thoughts linking the situation and the emotion

The next time you are aware of being distressed as a result of your work situation, you are encouraged to complete this first step (identifying the situation, emotion and thoughts) on the form on the next page, which was also described earlier in the detection section of the book, by asking yourself the questions listed below:

- What was the situation?
- What happened?
- What feelings did I have?
- What thoughts did I have?
- What was going through my mind when I began to feel upset in this situation?
- What meaning did it have for me?
- Why was it a problem?

IDENTIFYING THE SITUATION, FEELINGS AND THOUGHTS

This form is intended to help you identify specific negative thoughts at times of upset and connect these with the trigger situation and specific emotions you experience. When you are upset or as soon after as you can, fill out the following 3 columns going from left to right.

Feelings	Situation	Thoughts
What was I feeling? How bad was the feeling? (0-100)	Where was I? What was going on?	What went through my mind? What did it mean to me?

Identifying the effects of thinking: It's useful to look at the effects that certain thoughts or thinking processes can have in both the emotional and the behavioral arenas. This serves two purposes:

- It helps us recognize how dysfunctional thinking can have significant effects on both therapists as well as clients.
- It provides a motivation to test and revise this thinking to a more healthy and functional set of cognitions.

The steps involved are as follows:

- Identify a thought from an analysis of those which arise when negative feelings are elicited by a therapy situation. For example, supposing you identified the thought, "This client doesn't want to get better" or, "This person is deliberately sabotaging my efforts."

Now ask yourself the following questions:

- What is the effect on me of having these thoughts?
- What effect does it have on my emotions?
- What effect does it have on my behavior within therapy and outside?

In the above example it may become obvious that these thoughts probably lead to irritation and frustration (emotional consequences) and may also result in not working as hard with this client or being defensive and acting in an irritated manner, which may in turn influence the client's actions (behavioral consequences). Let's look at the costs and benefits of having the thoughts and beliefs you have identified about yourself, the client or therapy.

ANALYZING WHAT EFFECTS THESE THOUGHTS AND BELIEFS HAVE ON YOU

Identified thought/belief:

_____

_____

Degree of belief (0-100%) _____

Advantages of holding this belief	Disadvantages of holding this belief
How does it help me?	How does it hinder me?

IDENTIFYING THINKING DISTORTIONS

Having established that the thought is creating some costs (for example, interfering with therapy, upsetting you) we now move on to modifying or countering the thoughts by means of several standard CBT methods. In the same way that identifying distortions in thinking can help clients distance themselves from their thinking and begin reappraising their thoughts, the ability to recognize distorted thinking can also be very beneficial for care providers.

The steps involved are:

- Become familiar with the concept of cognitive distortions by reading "Cognitive Distortions: Eleven Ways to Make Yourself Miserable" on the next page.

- Identify tendencies to engage in any particular distortions by writing down some personal examples as suggested in this handout.

- Examine an identified thought or set of thoughts collected from a recent upsetting situation which you recorded on the Identifying the Situation, Feelings and Thoughts worksheet.

- Label which distortion(s), if any, is in evidence in this thought or set of thoughts. For example, "this client does not want to get better and is sabotaging me and the therapy" is an example of labeling and personalizing (blaming).

  The thought, "I am not doing good therapy, and this client will relapse" is an example of jumping to conclusions (fortune-telling and mental filter).

- Respond to the initial dysfunctional thought(s) which follows from the detection of distortions ("Since I know I am mind-reading I need to not assume but rather to get more information about what this client might be thinking"). In this example, the provider has now replaced the initial dysfunctional thought with an alternative cognitive response which is likely to be more helpful and functional. The following form can be used to record problem situations, feelings, thoughts and distortions as a means to facilitate cognitive reappraisal and reframing.

LEARNING ABOUT COGNITIVE DISTORTIONS (11 WAYS TO MAKE YOURSELF MISERABLE)

Cognitive distortions are inaccuracies in our thinking. We can think of our thoughts as representations of reality, sort of like a photograph. If we have a smudge on the lens of the camera, then the photo will show a picture that does not accurately represent what was in front of the camera. Even if the lens is clear but we take a picture of only part of an object, then the picture will not accurately portray the whole object. It is safe to assume that everyone engages in cognitive distortions at times, especially during times of distress. It can be very helpful to be able to identify distortions in your thinking, because once you have discovered the distortion, you will know how to correct it and feel better. Identifying your cognitive distortions is like diagnosing the thought problem. A good diagnosis usually points to a helpful remedy. Below is a list of eleven common distortions with examples of how they might occur. See if you can identify one or more ways that you have engaged in this kind of thinking.

All or Nothing/Black or White: Seeing things as though there were only two possible categories.

Example: If a situation turns out imperfectly, you see it as a total failure. You forget to buy one item on a shopping list and think, "Well, I really blew that trip." Can you think of an example of how you have used this distortion?

Try writing it down below:

_____

_____

Overgeneralizing: A negative event is seen as part of a never-ending pattern of defeat.

Example: When shopping you notice that your check-out line is moving very slowly and think, "Why do I always pick the slowest line?"

Your example:

_____

_____

Mental Filter: Seeing only negative aspects of a situation while screening out the positive aspects.

Example: You focus on a critical comment a client made while ignoring all the positive feedback you received.

Your example:

_____

_____

Jumping to Conclusions: Predicting things will go a certain way before you have the facts.

Example: You hear that the agency will be cutting back on staff, and you assume you will be among the first to go.

Your example:

_____

_____

Mind-Reading: Assuming that you know exactly what someone is or will be thinking about you.

Example: A colleague doesn't seem as friendly as usual and you think, "He must be angry with me."

Your example:

_____

_____

Fortune-telling: Predicting that things will turn out badly and that you won't be able to cope.

Example: Before going into a therapy session, you have an image of a client reacting negatively to something you say, and you assume that you will be bothered by this.

Your example:

_____

_____

Magnifying or Minimizing: Over-valuating or minimizing the importance of a situation or certain information.

Example: Even though you may be an effective helper, you are upset by the one client who terminated because he didn't feel he was being helped.

Your example:

_____

_____

Emotional Reasoning: Assuming that how you feel is an accurate reflection of how things are.

Example: If you are feeling anxious, you assume that something bad is going to happen.

Your example:

_____

_____

Shoulds: You tell yourself things "should" or "shouldn't" be a certain way. We do this with ourselves, with other people and situations. Variations of this can include "musts", "have to's" and other imperatives which sound like they come from some authority figure.

Example: "I shouldn't have done that" or, "I must prepare better for meetings."

Your example:

_____

_____

Labeling: This is an extreme form of all-or-nothing thinking which can be damaging to our self esteem and our relationships.

Example: Instead of simply acknowledging a mistake, we say, "I'm such a screw-up" (substitute "loser," "idiot," "jerk," etc.). Applying labels to ourselves or others ("that SOB") will tend to blind us to other qualities which we or others have.

Your example:

_____

_____

Personalizing (Blaming): This distortion creates enormous preventable suffering. It occurs when we hold ourselves responsible for something that isn't or wasn't entirely under our control. When this process is reversed, we blame someone else entirely for a situation we have a part in creating.

Example: Someone who noticed a colleague who didn't seem as friendly as usual thought, "I must have done something wrong."

Your example:

_____

_____

HOW TO RECOGNIZE DISTORTIONS IN YOUR THINKING

The next time you become upset or have a negative emotional reaction see if you can identify both what you were thinking and any distortions in the thoughts on this worksheet.

Feelings	Situation	Thoughts	Distortions
What was I feeling? How bad was the feeling? (0-100)	Where was I? What was going on?	What went through my mind?	Identify the distortion for each thought.

TESTING THE EVIDENCE

A procedure which allows providers to reality-test or check out the validity of their thoughts, when they involve assumptions or general conclusions, is described below. The steps involved are as follows:

- Identify the exact conclusion or assumption you are making (for example, the assumption that "I am an inadequate therapist" elicited by a client's relapsing or having a setback).

- Define the terms involved (in the example above, it may be important to know what would define an "adequate" or a "more than adequate" therapist). This step may reveal unrealistic expectations you might have.

- Ask what the level of belief in the thought is on a scale of 0-100. The importance of this step is that low-belief ratings can kick-start the process of seeing the other side (reasons why this thought is not valid or accurate). Also, this is a good baseline against which to later reassess the believability of these initial thoughts.

- List all the evidence which supports the assumption. In the above example, the data reviewed might include specific clients who have not done well or other indices of inadequate therapy.

- List evidence which goes against the assumption. In this same example, this might include clients who have reported positive outcomes and also any positive feedback received from referral agents and colleagues.

- Reconsider the original assumption and how much you now believe it. This cognitive intervention will often successfully challenge the over-generalized responding which occurs when an event is taken out of context.

- Decide if any further action is needed to test out the assumption or initial negative thought. For example, you might ask clients for feedback regarding their satisfaction with therapy.

The worksheet on the next page can be a very useful and systematic way of carrying out this kind of cognitive intervention, and we would encourage you to complete it if you become aware of strong negative thoughts underlying your distress.

SELF-HELP FORM

REVIEWING THE EVIDENCE FOR YOUR NEGATIVE THOUGHT(S)

Identified thought(s):

_____

_____

_____

_____

_____

_____

Degree of belief (0-100%) _____

Evidence for	Evidence against

Degree of belief in thought now (0-100%): _____

Action plan to further test the thought:

_____

_____

_____

_____

_____

_____

_____

GENERATING ALTERNATIVE VIEWPOINTS

This technique, also known as reattribution, can be helpful in evaluating negative, rigid and emotionally-arousing explanations of events by considering other less negative interpretations.

The steps involved are:

- Identify exactly how you are interpreting a stressful situation and what effect this interpretation is having. An example is a situation where a client is having a setback or relapse and you view this as a reflection of your not being competent enough. This interpretation can demoralize both you and the client to the extent that both this client's therapy, and the therapy you do in general, is rendered less effective.

- Brainstorm all other possible explanations. In the above example, looking at other factors which might have contributed to the event (the setback/lapse) might bring to light the fact that the client missed several doses of psychotropic medication, has had a lot of extra recent stress, was demoralized and was not following the plan discussed for how to deal with setbacks.

- Review the evidence to support each of these alternatives and estimate how likely it is that each contributed to the outcome.

- Come up with a more sophisticated and comprehensive explanation for what happened based on the above.

- Problem-solve what can be done to address these issues. In the above example, possible solutions may include facilitating greater client compliance with medication and psychotherapy, targeting the additional stress, working on the demoralization cognitively or checking into other therapeutic interventions in addition to what has already been implemented.

The worksheet on the next page will be helpful in facilitating the use of this cognitive technique.

GENERATING ALTERNATIVE WAYS OF LOOKING AT THINGS BESIDES THE INITIAL THOUGHT

Identified thought: _____

_____

Degree of belief (0-100%) _____

List all other possible viewpoints or explanations	What is the evidence for this?

Degree of belief in original thought now (0-100%): _____

Is more information needed to decide which of the above is more likely or logical? Yes _____
No _____

If so, how could this be obtained?

Action plan: _____

_____

_____

_____

_____

DECATASTROPHIZING AND DE-AWFULIZING

If the thoughts identified in your analysis of distressing situations involves some "what if" or "worst case scenario" thinking, this technique can help:

1. More realistically assess how likely this scenario actually is to happen.
2. Consider how bad the consequences would be if it did actually happen.

The steps involved are:

- Identify what future negative outcomes are being predicted. For example, after meeting a new client and suspecting that her diagnosis might be borderline personality disorder, you might have the following automatic thoughts (linked with negative emotions): "This will be draining, she will be manipulative, suicidal, demanding and angry; I won't be able to do effective therapy."

- Consider how likely it is that each of these will actually occur (de-catastrophizing). In the above example, you might make the following re-appraisal: "In my experience, not all borderline clients act this way. I can recall some who didn't. How likely is it both from the research and from my prior experience that I won't be able to be effective to some extent in some areas?"

- Consider the worst outcome and what the consequences would be (de-awfulizing).

- How awful would it actually be if that did happen?

- What coping strategies could be used to deal with it?

In the example above, you might ask yourself, "Even if this client does act in all these ways, what then? How would I handle it therapeutically and personally? Even if I couldn't do standard therapy, what could I do?"

By doing this kind of review, it often becomes apparent that you might be assuming the worst (which may not happen) and, even if it did, you actually have a number of resources to deal with it effectively. This will lead to a reduction in emotional distress.

The worksheet on the next page may help to explore the probabilities and consequences of negative predictions. If you fill it out systematically, when these anxiety-provoking situations come up, it will facilitate both de-catastrophizing and de-awfulizing.

DE-CATASTROPHIZING WHEN THINKING THE WORST

My worst fear	How likely is this to happen? (0-100%)	What would I do if it did happen? How would I cope?	What is the most likely outcome?

PUTTING IT ALL TOGETHER (ADAPT)

All or some of the techniques which have been outlined in this section may prove to be helpful when a care provider is experiencing strong emotional or cognitive reactions which are associated with impairment in the emotional or behavioral arenas. A useful self-help method of dealing with episodes of emotional distress experienced in being a caregiver, more generally in the workplace or in one's personal life using some well-known cognitive behavioral procedure, is contained in the acronym ADAPT, which is described below and in more detail in Ludgate (2012). This procedure summarizes the key steps a provider can use in applying CBT in a way which facilitates self-help.

The acronym ADAPT stands for:

- **A**ctivating events and triggers
- **D**etecting feelings
- **A**nswering thoughts
- **P**roceeding adaptively
- **T**esting outcome

USING THE **ADAPT** FORMAT TO DEAL WITH DISTRESS AND ASSOCIATED NEGATIVE THOUGHTS

Activating event or trigger

What are the stressful situations I am encountering (work-related, non work-related)?_____

_____

Detecting feelings and thoughts

What are my emotions? _____

What are my physical feelings? _____

What are my key thoughts and beliefs relating to these situations? _____

_____

What is the effect of my thinking on my emotions and behavior?_____

_____

What are some core beliefs about my role as a provider or in general which are influencing my thinking in these situations? _____

_____

Answering thoughts

What is the evidence for and against my thoughts? _____

_____

What are other ways I could look at this? _____

_____

What is the worst that could happen and how likely is this? _____

_____

What would I do if the worst did happen? _____

_____

Proceeding adaptively

What can I do or how can I think which will help me deal more effectively with this current situation? _____

_____

_____

_____

What can I do in general to reduce my current level of distress?_____

_____

Who might I reach out to?_____

_____

Test the outcome

What has changed in how I feel or how I am acting differently since I came up with or proceeded with the plan noted above? _____

_____

_____

Is it working?_____

_____

If not, what else might I do?_____

_____

Some readers may recognize in the prior worksheet some of the strategies they use with clients.

It is time to start practicing what we preach!

Acceptance strategies

As mentioned previously, providers sometimes are guilty of trying too hard to control situations which cannot be controlled. In this category would be certain client behaviors and our own human reactions including those of anxiety, irritability etc. In the section on CBT as self-therapy, we described ways of checking into and changing thinking patterns that may lead to emotional distress or upset. This can be a useful way of catching emotion on the way up and preventing it from becoming more severe. However, in some situations, like those mentioned above, the problem becomes one of dealing with the unpleasant realities of unappreciative or angry clients, situations such as terminal or unremitting disorders and feelings in ourselves of frustration, disappointment and irritation. This requires an attitude which accepts the way things are (the client who does not follow through on exercise or diet recommendations despite health consequences) rather than how they *should* be (the perfectly compliant client with consistent progress towards the treatment goals). Instead of taking things like this personally, we might see that this is almost to be expected in some cases and try to understand the reasons why. When faced with our own stress reactions as health providers, we might appreciate the universality of the hazards we face and accept the inevitable distress (which hopefully we can also counter using some of the methods described in this workbook) rather than rail against the situation or blame ourselves for being weak for feeling this way.

Acceptance does not imply passive resignation (which might be a sign of burnout). Rather, it is the first stage in helping ourselves to accept what is, and our own reaction to it, while also looking to find ways to cope or problem-solve around the issues (what can I do about the stress, which I do not blame myself for having, how can I motivate this client to change while not judging him for not doing this up to now?). The issue of knowing when to accept and when to try to change situations is, of course, summed up beautifully in the Serenity Prayer, which many are familiar with:

> *God grant me the serenity to accept the things I cannot change,*
> *The courage to change the things I can,*
> *And the wisdom to know the difference.*

A similar piece of wisdom is also contained in a Mother Goose rhyme which advises that for "every ailment under the sun, there be remedy or there be none. If there be one, try to find it. If there be none, never mind it."

Mindfulness and compassion

Related to the importance of acceptance is mindfulness. Mindfulness consists of a focused awareness of the present moment without judgment or evaluation. This is rather different from what we often do, which is to go to the past or the future or make judgments or valuations about what is happening now. Let's suppose that I am watching a beautiful sunset. If I am in a mindful state I would really experience all aspects of the sunset, how it looks, how I feel right in this moment. This is likely to be a fuller and more enriching experience than if I start to think, "This sunset better hurry up; I have so much to do later" or "This is nice, but doesn't even compare to the sunset I saw in Key West last year." These kinds of past or future comparisons or associated evaluative thoughts detract from the experience.

> Mindfulness consists of a focused awareness of the present moment without judgment or evaluation.

Now let's think about what might happen when I am upset by a work situation such as a client arriving 20 minutes late for our session. Using a mindful approach, I might become aware of feelings of irritability or of being pressed for time and stressed but, importantly, I simply observe these feelings and the fact that we now have less time because of the late start. But I do not add in judgments or evaluations such as: "He is doing this deliberately and doesn't respect me" or, "I should not get upset by this," which only serves to make the situation worse. Kelly Wilson, in his important book, *Mindfulness for Two* (2008), speaks to the need not just to help our clients learn mindfulness strategies to improve their mental health but also the importance of the provider or therapist using the same principles while working with these same clients. In this way we increase our awareness of what is going on in therapy but with an observing rather than a judgmental stance.

So if a client becomes angry with you, for example, rather than have a reflexive evaluative reaction ("That jerk...how dare he?") you could instead pay attention to exactly what is being said to you, what tone of voice is being used, what you are feeling somatically and emotionally and so on. This observer stance with no judgments of either the other person or ourselves is intrinsic to being more effective as helpers since the water is not muddied by judgments, labels and evaluations, and it also reduces helper distress. Mindfulness and how to practice it is described clearly in Kabat-Zinn (2005) *Coming to Our Senses: Healing Ourselves and the World Through Mindfulness.*

Compassion to Ourselves and Others

So what would be entailed in a self-compassionate approach? Compassion involves three major dimensions:

1. Kindness: Understanding one's difficulties and being kind to oneself in the face of problems rather than being judgmental and self-critical.
2. Common humanity: Seeing one's experiences as part of the human condition (and in this case also the health provider's condition!) rather than personal, isolated and shaming.
3. Mindful acceptance: Awareness and acceptance of painful thoughts and feelings rather than over-identifying with them.

It is recommended that if something has distressed or upset you at work or in a non-work situation you might go through the following steps:

- Note the feelings.
- Accept how you feel (tell yourself, "it's okay to feel this way") and refuse to judge yourself for feeling like this.
- Bring to mind that many people like you experience these same emotions.
- Put yourself in compassionate self mode and feel empathy for your upset self ("I am struggling with a tough situation").
- Adopt a compassionate body posture (sometimes a hand on your own shoulder or a gentle rubbing similar to what a good friend or partner might do) and a soft, sympathetic tone of voice when you speak to yourself.

- Ask yourself what you can do at this point to soothe yourself or take care of the issue (problem-solve).

Note: Self-compassion is not the same as self-pity which does not have an action or problem-solving component. It is also much healthier than the strident self-criticism or shaming of ourselves that we often engage in. Chodron (1994) expresses this powerfully by stating that we, as practitioners, need to have compassion for our own wounds and never give up on ourselves as only then can we have unconditional compassion for others and never give up on them. A tremendous aspiration for all of us providers and helpers!

EXERCISE

HOW ARE YOU WITH ACCEPTANCE AND COMPASSION AND WHAT MORE DO YOU NEED TO DO FOR YOU?

Do you need to become more accepting of yourself and situations you find yourself in?

Yes _____   No _____   I am already doing this _____

If yes, how might you do this? _____

_____

_____

Could you benefit from using mindfulness in your life and in your work?

Yes _____   No _____   I do this already_____

If yes, how might you make this happen? _____

_____

_____

Do you need to be more self-compassionate?

Yes_____   No_____   I already practice this_____

If yes, how and when might you do this?_____

_____

_____

What self-soothing activities might you engage in to accompany self-compassion when you are upset?

_____

_____

_____

PEER INTERVENTIONS

On a road journey when we have car problems we may not be able to deal with these without some help from others. Similarly with our own issues, we may need to have some help from peers, supervisors or even professionals as required.

Supervision

Many providers attest to the importance of good supervision in their personal and professional development. Many feel that they learned more from supervisors concerning effective therapy than from hundreds of hours of didactic instruction. Beyond this is the invaluable added benefit of supervision; in that safe setting, therapists are able to address frustrations, anxieties and other emotional reactions to their work. The kind of supervision most likely to result in work stress reduction of the kind we are discussing is likely to be where the supervisor is a colleague or peer rather than someone in a position of greater power. It would seem that this power differential and consequent evaluation anxiety might compromise openness about more personal work-related struggles, and this spirit of openness is critical for distress reduction.

> Research shows that psychotherapists and other helpers find a good deal of nurturance from supervision, peer support groups, or informal peer contact.

Supervision is often aimed at either specific competence in a field like CBT, for state licensure, or for both. In either case there is usually is no fear of consequences on the supervisee's part with the possible exception of ethical violations in the latter situation. It is incumbent upon the supervisor to make it clear that the purpose of supervision is to provide a forum for the supervisee to discuss the rewards, frustrations, stressors and challenges both with clients and in the workplace in general and not just to improve their skill level or increase productivity. It is important that those of us who are in a supervisory role think of how we can facilitate better self-care. It needs to be mentioned, however, that supervision should not become personal therapy for the supervisee in a more general way. If the supervisee needs to use supervision to "recharge the batteries" and find ways to feel less demoralized in the work place this can be a legitimate focus of supervision. If supervision is being used to deal with partner or family concerns, personal therapy should be recommended and help with a referral offered.

If no supervision is provided or required in your agency or if you work in solo practice, it is advisable to seek out some informal peer supervision for yourself. The benefits of having collegial support as well as having consultation on clinical issues can be considerable.

Peer support

In any agency, it is highly desirable that there be a forum where colleagues can talk not just about cases but about other issues including their own frustrations. Agency directors could facilitate this and, additionally, make these meetings more meaningful by making sure they are peer-led (no power differential) and in a safe atmosphere with no fear of consequences for honest reflection. Ideally, such meetings might be held out of the office. If not, a provided lunch might be helpful as will an open agenda where individuals can seek support, guidance and normalization related to work stresses. It should be a legitimate use of this time to report on feeling time-pressured and overworked and not just engage in case discussion.

The invitation to enter the open door of a colleague and ask for some help can be a wonderful antidote to work stress, and we would encourage you to avail yourself of this and also to offer it to colleagues, especially those joining a practice or new to the many stresses inherent in our work. In solo practice, which can be a lonely existence, it may be necessary to seek out other colleagues in a similar position to discuss shared difficulties and find a forum for mutual support and encouragement.

Reaching out to troubled peers

How can we do a better job detecting when a colleague needs help? Sometimes we are so enmeshed in our own daily lives and attending to the demands of our work that we fail to see that a peer or colleague is struggling. Since we are trained to be observers of mood shifts or anxiety, we ought to be able to pick up on changes in a colleague's behavior or observed mental state and broach it with them.

Our reticence to intervene is often due to a distorted way of thinking. It is highly unlikely that a colleague would be offended by hearing you say (in private) something like, "I say this out of concern and caring, and I might be off-base, but you do not seem like yourself these days. Is everything okay and can I do anything?" Ask yourself whether you would be offended by this or whether you would see it as an indication of regard and caring.

It has been shown (Woods et al., 1985) that 32% of therapists suffer from burnout and depression to a serious enough degree as to impair them in their work, and 26% perceive this in colleagues. The key question is what these individuals do after noticing problems.

While impairment and mental health issues in providers is clearly a matter for action by our professional organizations, our licensing boards and employee assistance programs, it is the responsibility of all of us to keep a keen eye out for distress in peers and colleagues and to act compassionately and proactively when we see that they are struggling

ORGANIZATIONAL INTERVENTIONS

"Not giving these workers help can undermine not only an organization but its long-term mission. If we don't do something about compassion fatigue we are going to lose people."
—C. Figley

Caregiver stress can affect the workplace in many ways. It's surprising how fast and far caregiver stress can spread. Toxic attitudes can be infectious and damaging. Impacts include:

- Greater staff turnover
- Increased tardiness and absenteeism
- More worker's compensation and health insurance claims
- Friction between employees and management
- Negative attitudes among staff
- Lower morale
- Rigidity and inflexibility among employees
- Diminished sense of a future vision
- More ethical violations
- Less respect for clients

There are several things that employers can do to minimize the risk that their workplaces will be further damaged by caregiver stress. They include:

- Provide adequate training about caregiver stress
- Address this issue in regular staff meetings
- Encourage peer support, both formal and structured, and informal and unstructured
- Provide workspaces that allow for privacy, confidentiality and a calm and pleasant work environment
- Provide employee assistance program services
- Promote counseling and support for employees
- Develop mentoring programs
- Provide outside consultation and training on worker wellness, caregiver stress and self-care
- Raise awareness of good self-care practices
- Monitor staff workloads
- Promote good relationships among staff
- Have an open door policy and encourage feedback
- Have solid personal safety plans in place
- Encourage teamwork
- Address and resolve staff conflict
- Offer opportunities for training, education and advancement

If you're noticing signs of caregiver stress in yourself, there are some specific things you can do at work that may help relieve some of those concerns:

- Diversify your caseload (if possible) to reduce your contact with severely traumatized people
- Make sure you are getting adequate supervision and support
- Use your coworkers to help debrief and manage your symptoms
- Take action to help not only yourself, but others at work who may also be struggling

CHECKLIST

How Healthy is Your Workplace?

Workplaces can be breeding grounds for unhealthy attitudes and low morale. Consider some of these workplace characteristics and assess how your organization is doing.

_____ Our workforce is stable and doesn't have too much turnover

_____ Most of the employees have solid attendance and show up on time

_____ Supervisors and administrators show respect for front-line staff

_____ Employees generally have positive attitudes

_____ Morale is good

_____ We keep our mission in clear focus

_____ We consistently show respect toward those we serve

_____ For the most part, employees have clear and appropriate boundaries

_____ The well-being of the staff is important to the agency

_____ We talk about self-care on a regular basis

_____ We usually do a good job of supporting each other and helping share the load

_____ It's important in our culture for us to support each other personally and professionally

_____ We try to maintain a pleasant work environment, both for ourselves and for those we serve

_____ Employees are encouraged to seek counseling, health care and employee assistance programs

_____ Caregiver stress, self-care and wellness are emphasized

_____ I feel safe at work

_____ We have healthy ways of resolving conflict

_____ I have opportunities to learn new things and advance in my career

PROFESSIONAL INTERVENTIONS

For a small number of individuals the level of distress reaches an unsustainable level of severity where professional help may be desirable or even necessary. Surveys have shown that up to 60% of professional helpers may experience clinical depression at some time in their lives, which is significantly above the rates found in the general population (Epstein &Bower, 1997). Additionally, these authors report that one in four will experience suicidal thoughts, and one in 16 will make suicide attempts. Moreover, divorce rates are significantly higher for mental health professionals. It is not always clear which comes first, the work or the distress. Do individuals with pre-existing psychological disorders seek out the care giving field in an attempt to better understand themselves? Does helping others or working in this field create burnout, compassion fatigue and distress in some individuals who are otherwise well-adjusted? Either way, care givers who are suffering may need personal therapy or counseling if the other less intensive interventions presented in this book aren't sufficient.

Since confidentiality and other practical issues regarding seeking help in a particular geographical area can interfere, it is important that professional groups be forward-thinking and consider how best to help impaired or struggling colleagues.

A lot can be learned in this regard from how impaired physicians' and lawyers' programs are set up and operated. National associations have been somewhat slow to explore these possibilities but, as members of local and national organizations, we should put our full weight behind any initiatives to provide immediate and confidential help to colleagues to both prevent personal distress and ultimately to benefit clients by ensuring healthier, better adjusted providers. We need to create a climate, not just of acceptance, but of reinforcement, for individuals who seek help or those who endeavor to help colleagues who are struggling.

In this regard it has been inspirational to have leaders in our field such as Vicky Rippere, Ruth Williams, and others going back some years (Rippere & Williams, 1985) speak openly and bravely of their own struggles with depression and other issues. More recently, it has been gratifying to see a number of therapists contribute to the book, *Breaking the Silence: Mental Health Professionals Disclose their Personal and Family Experiences with Mental Illness* (2008) edited by Stephen Hinshaw. We both have great respect for providers we know who have sought out therapy with us or other providers and hopefully you, the reader, would not hesitate to take this step were it obvious that you needed to.

When is professional help indicated?

1. When self-directed or other less intensive efforts have not reduced significant levels of distress.
2. When symptoms are severe and continuous and impact personal, social and occupational functioning.
3. When safety becomes an issue associated with clinical depression, hopelessness, demoralization or reckless, self-destructive behavior.
4. When trusted colleagues, peers, family or friends are worried enough to suggest the need for professional interventions.

WHEN WOULD YOU SEEK PROFESSIONAL HELP, AND WHAT MIGHT HOLD YOU BACK?

Whether you have ever had counseling in the past or not, take a few minutes to consider the following;

Would I go for professional help if I need to it the future?   Yes _____   No_____

If yes, under what circumstances?_____
_____
_____

If no, what would hold you back?_____
_____
_____

Can you think of any thoughts or beliefs that might prevent you doing this?   Yes _____   No _____

If so, what beliefs would interfere? _____
_____
_____

How could you counter these using ideas from this book or other places? _____
_____
_____

Chapter 6
Prevention

*"I have always been better at caring for and looking after others than
I have been in caring for myself. But in these later years I made progress."*
—C. Rogers

We know that prevention can dramatically minimize the negative impact of caregiver stress. Preventive factors that have been shown to be helpful include:

- Strong social support (both in personal life and work life)
- Balancing work and home life
- Finding satisfaction and purpose in your work
- Limiting exposure to trauma when possible
- Practicing good self-care
- Using supervision
- Building peer support
- Obtaining training and education about caregiver stress
- Being appropriately self-aware

PERSONAL STRATEGIES FOR PREVENTION

Compassion satisfaction

We've talked a good bit about the challenges of being in the business of helping others. By this point, you may be wondering what the upside of this work is. You probably aren't doing this for the money, so you may be wondering why you're still in the field when there are emotional risks to this work. You may experience just enough of the compassion satisfaction, or the good part of being a helper, that you keep showing up for work. Compassion satisfaction is the notion that there are positive things that come out of helping, and that those experiences can help tide us over during the stressful parts of this work.

> Compassion satisfaction is the notion that there are positive things that come out of helping, and that those experiences can help tide us over during the stressful parts of this work.

Compassion satisfaction is the pleasure you derive from being able to do your work well. You may feel positively about:

- Your colleagues
- Your ability to contribute to the work setting
- Working toward the greater good of society
- Helping others through your work
- The helper's high—those moments when you really feel that you are in the right place at the right time, and that what you are doing is making a difference

With compassion satisfaction, you may feel:

- Able to handle new protocols and technology
- Successful and happy with your work
- A desire to continue to engage in your work
- Satisfied and invigorated by the act of helping
- Pleasure with the progress of your clients
- Optimistic about your ability to make a difference

Building resilience

> You can think of resilience as the ability to return to the original form or position after being bent, compressed or stretched.

An important thing you can do to prevent caregiver stress and increase compassion satisfaction is to work on building your resilience. You can think of resilience as the ability to return to the original form or position after being bent, compressed or stretched. Picture a young tree in strong winds. That sapling is able to survive because it has the flexibility that allows it to return to its original form when the winds calm down. Resilience is not a fixed trait that you are either born with or not. You can work on developing greater flexibility and resilience. Just as you might exercise to build muscle you can focus on strengthening your ability to bounce back from difficult times. You can also think of resilience as elasticity or the ability to thrive when confronted by adversity. It's a positive adaptation to stress or trauma.

So where do you start? What can you work on to help build this essential trait in yourself? Here's a list of things you could focus on as you exercise your "resilience muscle":

- Resourcefulness
- Social support
- Compassion with healthy detachment
- Having vision, goals, purpose
- Altruism
- Emotional hardiness and flexibility
- Humor
- Optimism and hope
- Tolerating difficult experiences that help you overcome stress
- Flexibility, open mindedness and adaptability
- Actively facing fears and trying to solve problems
- Healthy, accurate self-esteem
- Spirituality
- Ability to use cognitive coping skills, not just emotional ones
- Willingness to seek meaning in stressful events
- Repeated exposure to minimal or moderate stressors to build resilience

> Just as we can experience vicarious trauma we can also experience vicarious resilience.

Vicarious resilience

Not all of our experience with traumatized people brings negative consequences. There are some pretty powerful and positive aspects of being around people who hurt. Just as we can experience vicarious trauma we can also experience vicarious resilience. We can learn about overcoming adversity from the trauma survivors we work with. Our empathetic engagement with suffering people is not always negative. We can experience positive transformation and empowerment through watching others and how they respond positively through trying times. We can develop an enhanced sense of hope and meaning and find a greater ability to put our own stressors into perspective.

> We can experience positive transformation and empowerment through watching others and how they respond positively through trying times.

Qualitative studies of interviewers of Holocaust survivors and clinicians working with torture survivors demonstrate vicarious resilience. In spite of hearing horrific tales from these traumatized people, the impact was not all negative. These workers noted an increased appreciation for their own lives, an awareness of the resilience and strength of the survivors, and a greater sense of justice and sensitivity to prejudice. They were also able to more fully appreciate their own freedoms, they saw their problems as being less severe and more manageable, they had a greater ability to positively reframe situations, and they experienced stronger motivation to contribute to the fight for human rights.

Creating a self-care plan

"A little nonsense now and then is relished by the wisest men."
—R. Dahl

Do you recall the quote by Remen that said that it's unrealistic to expect that we can walk through water and not get wet? On the surface that appears to be true. Of course we'll get wet if we walk through water. That seems like a no-brainer. However, it *is* possible to stay dry while walking through water. We can do that if we are protected. If we anticipate that we'll be walking through water we can prepare for it. We can wear a wet suit, we can put on fishing waders or we can pull on rain boots. We can be surrounded by water and not end up waterlogged if we have a solid self-care plan in place.

> It makes a lot more sense to plan daily, affordable, realistic activities as part of a self-care plan. Practical and do-able ideas are more likely to be done regularly anyway.

Once you've determined that you have some symptoms of caregiver stress you may wonder what on earth you can do about it. Your optimism may be waning and you may fantasize about quitting your job and leaving the field all together!

Before you throw in the towel on your current career you may want to develop a personalized self-care plan that will help pull you out of the slump you are experiencing. When you're looking at developing a self-care plan you want to think about the following:

- What has helped you feel refreshed and renewed in the past?
- Are there things you used to enjoy doing that you've let slip away?
- What brings you pleasure and joy?

Some of us have a pretty limited self-care plan...vacation! Unfortunately, vacations don't come around often enough, they can be costly and they aren't always peaceful and restorative. Many of us find that the week leading up to vacation is crammed full of things that must be done before leaving. As many of you have no doubt experienced, coming back to the office after time away can be so demanding that the afterglow of vacation quickly fades.

It makes a lot more sense to plan daily, affordable, realistic activities as part of a self-care plan. Practical and do-able ideas are more likely to be done regularly anyway.

Here is a chart (Skovholt and Trotter-Mathison, 2011) that compares three different studies of what self-care activities therapists found most helpful. This chart may give you some ideas for things you might include in your self-care plan.

Table 4:   Three Studies of Therapists' Self-Care Activities

Study 1: Top 10 Helpful Activities[a]	Study 2: Top 10 Career-Sustaining Behaviors[b]	Study 3: 234 Well-Functioning Psychologists' Top 10 Activities Contributing to Well Functioning[c]
Utilize close friends, significant others, or family as a source of support	Spending time with partner/family	Self-awareness and self-monitoring
Seek solutions to difficulties	Maintaining balance between professional and personal lives	Personal values
Use humor	Maintaining a sense of humor	Preserving balance between personal and professional lives
Choose internship activities of interest	Maintaining self-awareness	Relationship with spouse, partner, or family
Maintain self-awareness of the impact my internship experiences has on me and my work	Maintaining professional identity	Personal therapy
Seek out pleasurable diversions outside of internship	Engaging in quiet leisure activities	Relationships with friends
Consult with my fellow interns	Maintaining a sense of control over work responsibilities	Vacations
Set realistic goals for myself regarding internship	Engaging in physical activities	Professional identity
Seek supervision from clinical supervisor	Taking regular vacations	Informal peer support
Work to create a comfortable work environment for myself	Perceiving clients' problems as interesting	Mentor

[a] *Source:* "Intern Self-Care: An Exploratory Study into Strategy Use and Effectiveness," by J. A. Turner, L. M. Edwards, I. M. Eicken, K. Yokoyama, J. R. Castro, A. N. Tran, and K. L. Haggins, 2005, *Professional Psychology: Research and Practice, 36,* pp. 674-680.
[b] *Source:* "Career-Sustaining Behaviors, Satisfactions, and Stresses of Professional Psychologists," by P. Stevanovic and P. A. Rupert, 2004, *Psychotherapy: Theory, Research, Practice, Training, 41,* pp. 301-309.
[c] *Source:* "Well-Functioning in Professional Psychologists," J. J. Coster and M. Schwebel, 1997, *Professional Psychology: Research and Practice, 28,* pp. 5-13.

A study by Gamble, Pearlman, Lucca, and Allen (1994) lists what activities professionals found most helpful. Perhaps not surprisingly, taking a vacation topped the list! While that is usually a fun and refreshing thing to do, most of us are limited in doing that by both time and finances. The list includes the following items, along with the mean score (with a 6 being "extremely helpful").

4.60	Vacation	3.00	Aerobic exercise
4.34	Social activities	2.87	Attempted to diversify caseload
4.21	Emotional support from colleagues	2.14	Community involvement
4.10	Reading for pleasure	2.04	Relaxation exercises
4.06	Sought consultation with difficult cases	1.86	Gardening
3.91	Read relevant professional literature	1.51	Artistic expression
3.88	Took breaks during a workday	1.29	Spiritual practice
3.83	Emotional support from friends or family	1.17	Personal psychotherapy
3.78	Spent time with children	.95	Massage or bodywork
3.70	Listened to music	.88	Meditation
3.67	Spent time in nature	.56	Journal writing
3.59	Attended workshop or conference	.52	Yoga

Skovholt and Trotter-Mathison (2011) have come up with a list of things that sustain us in our work as well as a list of what depletes us in our work. Take a look at these lists and see if you're doing enough to sustain yourself, and see if you are doing things that end up depleting yourself.

Table 5: Factors That Sustain and Deplete the Professional Self

Factors That Sustain the Professional Self	Factors That Deplete the Professional Self
Joy in participating in others' growth	Feeling unsuccessful in helping the other
Feeling successful in helping others	Professional boundaries that allow for excessive other-care and too little self-care
Closely observing human life (creativity, courage, ingenuity, tolerance of pain) and meaningful human contact	Low peer support
Finely tuned professional boundaries	Low supervisor support
Peer support	High organizational conflict
Supervisor support	Excessive seriousness in purposes and style
Low level of organizational conflict	Little attention to long-term professional development
Sense of humor and playfulness	Inability to accept any ambiguous professional loss or normative failure
Constant focus on professional development and avoidance of stagnation and pseudo development	Neglecting the importance for self and others of a positive closure experience at the time of professional separation
Tolerance of some ambiguous professional loss and normative failure	Insufficient salary and benefits or educational credits if the practitioner is in training
Attempting to have a closure experience at the time of professional separation that is positive for both parties	Realism and idealism as one
Sufficient salary and benefits or educational credits if the practitioner is in training	Distinguishing between idealism and realism

Here's some food for thought. Who is responsible for your self-care? Think carefully...it's YOU. You are the only person who can do this. Only you can come up with ideas about what constitutes a solid self-care plan for you. And you are the only one who can implement your self-care plan. Yet so many of us are uncomfortable with self-care or even appropriate caretaking by others.

A possible barrier to prioritizing good self-care may be a dichotomy of our own making. We may feel that we must choose *either* meeting the needs of those we serve *or* taking care of ourselves. Rather than accepting this false dichotomy of either/or, maybe we should choose a both/and approach. We can do good work with others *and* keep ourselves well and healthy. It may even help to reframe that false dichotomy into a logical order in which we approach our work. We can take care of ourselves first so we can then take care of others. Even Mother Teresa recognized the potential drain of helping and made it mandatory for her nuns to take extended periods of time off to heal from the effects of their care giving. While extended furloughs or sabbaticals aren't something most of us can enjoy, we *can* make self-care a priority.

Leaving work at the office

A lot of us have trouble leaving work at work. It follows us home, if not in our briefcases then maybe it comes home with us on our phones, our laptops or *in our minds*. It's hard to shake off a tough day at work, and it's really tough when you've been trying to support hurting people all day long. It really helps to be intentional and deliberate in your transition home. Here are some ideas that may help with your transition home:

- Deal with outstanding issues: complete or delegate.
- Check in with on-call staff and say your goodbyes.
- Use your time going home to begin thinking of home and what your evening may look like.
- Pick a geographic point on your way home and decide that once you pass that spot you are done thinking about work. Shift gears to start thinking of home.
- Try not to take work home or, if you must, confine it to a certain time and place. You don't want to see work spread out on your bed or nightstand.
- Take off your name tag (hopefully when you get home the people there will recognize you without it).
- Note what you did well during the day.
- Change out of your work clothes when you get home.
- Play with your dog or child.
- Go for a walk outside.

Stress and self-care

You could probably guess that stress contributes to our pleasure, or lack of pleasure, in our work. Stress comes from all directions.

Sources of stress:

- Clients
- Supervisors
- Employer/agency

- Insurance/managed care
- Coworkers
- Failures
- Internal expectations
- External pressures

We can think of stress as physical or emotional strain. We can stress an object, and we can stress our minds. If you look up a dictionary definition of stress you'll see it described something like this:

- To pull or stretch to the breaking point
- To exert or strive to the utmost
- To injure by overexertion
- Great effort, tension, or pressure

You can see how this could refer to physical or mental strain. Picture a rubber band stretched between the index fingers on your left and your right hands. It's not useful when it's limp, with no pressure on it. Pull on it a bit so it becomes a bit stretched and taut. Now it's more useful. When you apply some stress it's able to do its job of holding things together.

If you pull harder, really stress it, you may find yourself cringing a bit. If you continue to exert pressure you know that at some point it will snap. You don't exactly know at what moment it will burst, or in what direction. But you do know it can't hold up under the increasing pressure. Scary, right? Keep that visual in mind when you find your internal pressures building. It may help you pull back in your own life and release the pressure before you snap.

Stress isn't all bad. There is an upside to stress:

- It makes us more alert
- It keeps life exciting
- It's exhilarating
- It makes us feel energized
- It can sharpen our senses in some situations

There is a definite and well-established downside. Some of you know this from personal experience:

- Physical problems
- High blood pressure
- Unstable blood sugar
- Increased pain
- More illnesses, weakened immune system
- Increased use of alcohol, drugs, medications
- Sleep problems
- Irritability
- Relationship turmoil

Standards of Self-Care

The Green Cross Academy of Traumatology is an organization dedicated to the promotion of ethical trauma care. They offer guidelines for self-care, and suggest making a formal, tangible commitment to self-care: written, specific, and measurable. Review this document for ideas about how you can strengthen your own self-care practices.

I. Purpose of the Guidelines

As with the standards of practice in any field, the practitioner is required to abide by standards of self-care. These guidelines are utilized by all members of the Green Cross. The purpose of the guidelines is twofold: First, do no harm to yourself in the line of duty when helping/treating others. Second, attend to your physical, social, emotional, and spiritual needs as a way of ensuring high quality services for those that look to you for support as a human being.

II. Ethical Principles of Self-Care in Practice

These principles declare that it is unethical not to attend to your self-care as a practitioner because sufficient self-care prevents harming those we serve.

1. Respect for the dignity and worth of self: A violation lowers your integrity and trust.

2. Responsibility of self-care: Ultimately it is your responsibility to take care of yourself and no situation or person can justify neglecting it.

3. Self-care and duty to perform: There must be a recognition that the duty to perform as a helper cannot be fulfilled if there is not, at the same time, a duty to self-care.

III. Standards of Humane Practice of Self-Care

1. Universal right to wellness: Every helper, regardless of her or his role or employer, has a right to wellness associated with self-care.

2. Physical rest and nourishment: Every helper deserves restful sleep and physical separation from work that sustains them in their work role.

3. Emotional rest and nourishment: Every helper deserves emotional and spiritual renewal both in and outside the work context.

4. Sustenance modulation: Every helper must utilize self-restraint with regard to what and how much they consume (for example food, drink, drugs, stimulation) since it can compromise their competence as a helper.

IV. Standards for Expecting Appreciation and Compensation

1. Seek, find, and remember appreciation from supervisors and clients: These and other activities increase worker satisfactions that sustain them emotionally and spiritually in their helping.

2. Make it known that you wish to be recognized for your service: Recognition also increases worker satisfactions that sustain them.

3. Select one or more advocates: They are colleagues who know you as a person and as a helper and are committed to monitoring your efforts at self-care.

V. Standards for Establishing and Maintaining Wellness

Section A: Commitment to self-care

1. Make a formal, tangible commitment: written, public, specific, and measurable promises of self-care.
2. Set deadlines and goals: The self-care plan should set deadlines and goals connected to specific activities of self-care.
3. Generate strategies that work and follow them: Such a plan must be attainable and followed with great commitment and monitored by advocates of your self-care.

Section B: Strategies for letting go of work

1. Make a formal, tangible commitment: Written, public, specific, and measurable promise of letting go of work in off hours and embracing rejuvenation activities that are fun, stimulating, inspiriting, and generate joy of life.
2. Set deadlines and goals: The letting go of work plan should set deadlines and goals connected to specific activities of self-care.
3. Generate strategies that work and follow them: Such a plan must be attainable and followed with great commitment and monitored by advocates of your self-care.

Section C: Strategies for gaining a sense of self-care achievement

1. Strategies for acquiring adequate rest and relaxation: The strategies are tailored to your own interest and abilities which result in rest and relaxation most of the time.
2. Strategies for practicing effective daily stress reductions method(s): The strategies are tailored to your own interest and abilities in effectively managing your stress during working hours and off-hours with the recognition that they will probably be different strategies.

VI. Inventory of Self-Care Practice — Personal

Section A: Physical

1. Body work: Effectively monitoring all parts of your body for tension and utilizing techniques that reduce or eliminate such tensions.
2. Effective sleep induction and maintenance: An array of healthy methods that induce sleep and a return to sleep under a wide variety of circumstances including stimulation of noise, smells, and light.
3. Effective methods for assuring proper nutrition: Effectively monitoring all food and drink intake and lack of intake with the awareness of their implications for health and functioning.

Section B: Psychological

1. Effective behaviors and practices to sustain balance between work and play.
2. Effective relaxation time and methods.
3. Frequent contact with nature or other calming stimuli.
4. Effective methods of creative expression.
5. Effective skills for ongoing self-care:
    a. assertiveness
    b. stress reduction
    c. interpersonal communication

d. cognitive restructuring

e. time management.

6. Effective skill and competence in meditation or spiritual practice that is calming.

7. Effective methods of self-assessment and self-awareness.

Section C: Social/interpersonal

1. Social supports: at least five people, including at least two at work, who will be highly supportive when called upon.

2. Getting help: knowing when and how to secure help – both informal and professional – that will be delivered quickly and effectively.

3. Social activism: being involved in addressing or preventing social injustice that result in a better world and a sense of satisfaction for trying to make it so.

VII. Inventory of Self-Care Practice – Professional

1. Balance between work and home: devoting sufficient time and attention to both without compromising either.

2. Boundaries/limit setting: Making a commitment and sticking to regarding:
   a. time boundaries/overworking
   b. therapeutic/professional boundaries
   c. personal boundaries
   d. dealing with multiple roles (both social and professional)
   e. Realism in differentiating between things one can change and accepting the others.

3. Getting support/help at work through:
   a. peer support
   b. supervision/consultation/therapy
   c. role models/mentors.

4. Generating work satisfaction: by noticing and remembering the joys and achievements of the work.

VIII. Prevention Plan development

1. Review current self-care and prevention functioning.

2. Select one goal from each category.

3. Analyze the resources for and resistances to achieving goal.

4. Discuss goal and implementation plan with support person.

5. Activate plan.

6. Evaluate plan weekly, monthly, yearly with support person.

7. Notice and appreciate the changes.

CHECKLIST

SELF-CARE BRAINSTORMING

In this activity you are going to come up with ideas about things that could become part of your self-care. This list doesn't need to be polished and formal, a more loose and open-minded brainstorming approach is what we're aiming for. Try to come up with ideas that stimulate all five of your senses: seeing, hearing, touching, tasting and smelling. Look at the various realms of your life: physical, emotional, social and spiritual. We'll list some ideas to help you get started. Check the ones that might work for you.

Physical

_____ Healthy eating

_____ Good sleep (7-8 hours nightly would be great)

_____ Physical activity and exercise

_____ Invigorating and stimulating activities

_____ Monitor alcohol, nicotine, and caffeine use

_____ Massage

_____ Yoga

_____ Regular health care

_____ Stay home when you're sick!

_____ Take some breaks from technology...unplug

_____ Get some physical activity during your workday: go outside, walk around, stretch

_____ Drink plenty of fluids

(Add as many others as you want)

_____

_____

_____

_____

_____

Emotional

_____ Read

_____ Recognize that you can't do everything

_____ Set limits and enforce them

_____ Get counseling as needed

_____ Listen to music

_____ Learn something new

_____ Journal or write

_____ Laugh more

_____ Seek humor and fun

_____ Get outside

_____ Unplug

_____ Adjust your standards

_____ Do something creative or expressive

_____ Communicate clearly

_____ Ask for what you need

_____ Monitor your self-talk
_____ Practice mindfulness
_____ Take time away from the suffering and trauma of others
_____ Develop your sense of curiosity
_____ Internalize the rewards of helping people
_____ Have empathy for yourself, be as gentle with yourself as you urge others to be with themselves
_____ Regularly assess and track how you are doing with your own self-care
_____ Practice laughing at your own mistakes and don't always take yourself too seriously

(Add as many others as you want)

_____
_____
_____
_____
_____

Work

_____ Seek variety in your work roles
_____ Develop a support team of others in your field
_____ Keep a balanced view of yourself: You are neither the best nor the worst at what you do
_____ Save thank-you notes you receive
_____ Limit your exposure to trauma
_____ Adhere to solid professional and practice boundaries
_____ Remember that not everyone you help will get better
_____ Monitor cognitive distortions
_____ Look around your office, does it create the atmosphere you seek?
_____ Learn to delegate effectively
_____ Refine and expand your professional skills
_____ Learn something new or a new way of doing your work

(Add as many others as you want)

_____
_____
_____
_____
_____
_____

Social

_____ Connect with people
_____ Enjoy children and young people
_____ Play with your pets
_____ Ask for help and accept it
_____ Take a class for fun
_____ Volunteer (carefully!)
_____ Choose who you spend time with
_____ Support groups, 12-step programs
_____ Ask people close to you to help you stick with your self-care plan

(Add as many others as you want)

_____

_____

_____

_____

Spiritual

_____ Pray or meditate

_____ Read spiritual material

_____ Work on forgiveness

_____ Worship with others

_____ Develop a sense of gratitude

_____ Seek spiritual counsel

_____ Practice restorative solitude as needed

_____ Pursue the work that you feel called to do

_____ Allow yourself to be enriched by the strength you see in others, even (especially) during their trials

(Add as many others as you can)

_____

_____

_____

_____

WORKSHEET
SELF-CARE PLAN

List things that you enjoy, that relax you, invigorate you or that bring you pleasure. Be as creative as possible and list as many things as you can think of.

_____

_____

_____

_____

_____

_____

_____

_____

_____

_____

_____

_____

_____

For one week, try to do at least one of the items on your list each day. Do this intentionally with the sole purpose of relieving some stress and enjoying something pleasurable. Write down what you do each day so you can keep yourself on track and monitor your progress.

Monday_____

Tuesday_____

Wednesday_____

Thursday_____

Friday_____

Saturday_____

Sunday_____

By taking care of yourself you will reduce your risk of developing compassion fatigue and lower your stress level. You will become more effective in your work with people, and you will find refreshment in your life outside of work.

Organizational prevention strategies

It's a forward-thinking, proactive organization that comes up with good prevention strategies for its workers. Martha has recently been involved with one such organization. This is an international group that places workers in slum communities throughout Southeast Asia. She became familiar with them when her son and his wife joined and moved to India to live and work in a slum.

As she talked with leaders of the organization she found that they talked a lot about caregiver stress with their member candidates during the preparation phase before moving overseas. They were open to expanding their support for their workers and Martha was privileged to be a part of their plan.

At the organization's all-staff gathering in Thailand, she presented several sessions on caregiver stress. All of the members of the organization were encouraged to take part. Since that time they have worked together in a year-long emphasis on sustaining compassion. Each month, the teams in various countries are given information on different aspects of caregiver stress. They are provided handouts, discussion questions, resources and a video of highlighted points for them to watch and talk about in their teams.

Catherall (1995) suggests that preventive mechanisms should be in place before they are needed. This allows them to be employed in a prepared response mode rather than a hurried and disorganized reaction mode. It's helpful for agencies to include psychoeducation, preparedness and planning as part of their prevention plan. Agencies and organizations will benefit greatly if they accept that this work has risks, but those stressors should be recognized and staff should be well-supported in tangible ways.

What can agencies, institutions and organizations do to better support their employees? Figley (1989) has several suggestions that help when families are impacted by traumatic stress. They can be adapted to the "family" of an organization:

1. The stressors are accepted as real and legitimate.
2. The problem is viewed as an institutional problem and not as a problem that is limited to the individual.
3. The general approach to the problem is to seek solutions not to assign blame.
4. There is a high level of tolerance for individual disturbance.
5. Support is expressed clearly, directly and abundantly in the form of praise, commitment and affection.
6. Communication is open and effective. There are few sanctions against what can be said. The quality of communication is good; messages are clear and direct.
7. There is a high degree of cohesion.
8. There is considerable flexibility of roles; individuals are not rigidly restricted to particular roles.
9. Resources—material, social and institutional—are utilized efficiently.
10. There is not a subculture of violence (emotional outbursts are not a form of violence).
11. There is no substance abuse.

One of the most important things organizations can do to prevent caregiver stress is to talk about it. It really can start that simply. By talking about the risks of this work, employers can begin to make some changes that reduce worker risk. This can be a surprisingly supportive action that translates into a much healthier set of staff members.

Other ideas for organizations may include:

- Debriefing
- Peer support
- Managing work loads
- Providing opportunities for supervision and education
- Monitoring staff wellness
- Looking for ways to provide feedback about possible concerns in stressed workers
- Varying the assignments of employees.

Ochberg (1991) identifies three things that organizations can do to effectively prevent caregiver stress from developing.

1. Look at the unique ways that individuals can process their exposure to traumatic stress. Show respect for the needs of each individual.
2. Normalize the reactions that workers have following exposure to the suffering of others.
3. Empower employees to take part in their own paths to healing so they can maintain dignity and a sense of power and control.

Figley (1989) and Catherall (1995) bring up some other ideas that can help agencies prevent caregiver stress. These can be implemented in most any organization and tailored to meet the specific needs of the group.

1. Provide resources such as financial aid, health insurance, flexibility in work schedule, time off, change in job duties, and monitoring worker needs.
2. Coworkers can help by clarifying the insights that a worker has, listening with care and a lack of judgment, and accepting the reactions of the colleague.
3. Coworkers can also correct cognitive distortions that an affected worker is thinking and can help modify any mistaken self-blame that the worker is experiencing.
4. Colleagues can help a coworker reframe the trauma and their cognitions around it. This can help combat distortions that add to self-blame and guilt.
5. These interventions are particularly helpful when the supportive coworker can listen and support while remaining empathetic, even when the emotional intensity may be high.

What can organization and managers do?

There are many things that organizations can do to prevent caregiver stress from developing in workers. Pearlman and McKay (2008) came up with some effective suggestions that can be modified to fit many organizational needs. As you review this information, consider your own workplace and start imagining how your employer could adopt some of these ideas to better meet your needs and those of your coworkers. Perhaps you could take part in developing a prevention plan for your organization that might make your work life a lot more enjoyable and reduce your risk of developing troublesome symptoms of your own.

VICARIOUS TRAUMA: WHAT CAN ORGANIZATIONS AND MANAGERS DO?

Excerpted by CARE from *Understanding and Addressing Vicarious Trauma.* L. A. Pearlman and L. McKay (2008). Headington Institute. www.headington-institute.org. Reprinted with permission.

Some humanitarian workers feel that their own organization increases their vicarious trauma instead of helping reduce it! Your organization's policies and practices may be frustrating and make things feel unnecessarily complicated. But it's worth remembering that organizations and managers don't deliberately set out to make life more difficult for you and the people you are trying to help. Sometimes they don't make the best use of the limited time and resources available to them, and this impedes your ability to do your job as well as you'd like. Sometimes they are just facing many competing demands and don't have enough time or resources to do everything with the greatest care and consideration.

However, when humanitarian organizations take an active interest in staff well-being they take a big step toward addressing things that can contribute to vicarious trauma.

Even in crisis situations there is a lot that organizations and management can do to structure work rules and develop organizational cultures that help lessen vicarious trauma in their staff.

Basic Considerations for Organizations

Here are some basic considerations for organizations. These can lessen the risk of vicarious trauma by helping humanitarian workers feel supported, valued, competent, and connected:

1. Adequate salary and time off (including R&R) for all staff:
2. Sufficient orientation, professional training, and management supervision for staff to feel competent and supported in their jobs:
3. Plans for staff safety (including security training and briefing on security protocols):
4. Access to medical and mental health support services including:
   - Health insurance
   - Information/training about the psychological and spiritual hazards of the work and effective self-care
   - Access to good confidential counseling support as needed: and
5. Support for families around issues such as child care, separation and relocation.

Organizational Culture and Work Roles

In addition, humanitarian workers will benefit from an organizational culture and work roles that are structured in ways that help prevent vicarious trauma by:

1. Encouraging connections, morale, and relationships, perhaps through some or all of the following:
   - Working in teams
   - Providing other avenues to connect with colleagues (e.g., social activities such as having lunch or occasional outings together)
   - Developing peer support networks
2. Encouraging communication and staff contributions by:

- Providing a voice in decision-making from and feedback to staff at all levels of the organizational hierarchy
- Providing information to help staff understand how and why decisions about resource allocations, deadlines, policies, and assignments are made
- Looking for ways to build diversity and job enrichment into the work
- Allowing for and actively encouraging staff to take adequate breaks during work

---

THINK ABOUT IT

- What are some things your organization already does well to support its staff and help reduce the risk of vicarious trauma?

- Are there some practical things you can think of that your organization could do better to support staff and reduce the risk of vicarious trauma:

  - During recruitment?

  - During orientation?

  - During employment?

- Upon leaving the organization?

What Managers Can Do

Are you a manager? Managers can take many steps to help lessen the impact of vicarious trauma on staff they are supervising. Here are some of them.

1. Understand the psychological and spiritual Impact of humanitarian work:

   - Be alert to how the cumulative exposure to stressful and traumatic situations may be affecting staff.

   - Regularly check in with staff about how they're coping—do not wait for them to approach you with a problem.

   - Support staff in seeking counseling or coaching if and when needed.

2. Set a good example in the way that you care for yourself, including:

   - Work at a sustainable and reasonable pace over time, and encourage staff you supervise to do the same.

   - Openly value things and people outside of work (e.g., time spent with your family)

   - Take allocated leave time

   - Acknowledge that humanitarian work can be challenging and that healthy work life balance takes practice and intentionality.

3. Especially during times of increased pressure or crises, look for ways to help staff keep current challenges in perspective by:

   - Reminding staff of the bigger picture of the organization's mission and purpose, and how this assignment or disaster response fits into that bigger picture

   - And reminding staff of the value the organization places upon them both as people and the organization's most important resources—the staff. Encourage the staff to work in sustainable ways. If that does not appear possible in the short-term, encourage them to take extra time after the immediate impact phase is over to rest and regain equilibrium.

4. Express concern for the general well-being of your staff and not just the quality of the work they are doing.

5. Make sure that staff suggestions and feedback about their jobs and the organization are heard and valued—even if you are fairly sure they will not result in tangible change in the near future.

6. Do not say or do things that would stigmatize staff who are struggling with vicarious trauma or other stress or trauma-related issues.

7. Strive to stay positive, and to praise and acknowledge effort and results whenever possible.

Managers can do many things to help lessen the impact vicarious trauma on staff they are supervising, including being a good example in how they maintain and care for themselves.

Some Final Words

We have found writing this workbook fulfilling and helpful in many ways, as we share a deep passion for this much-neglected topic. We sincerely hope the information and practical strategies in this workbook have helped you and will continue to assist you in this journey that all of us are on, where we are both attempting to *survive* and more importantly to *thrive* in our work as helpers and caregivers.

As we pointed out, the rewards are many and we wish you many of these. In addition, and on the flip side, stress is inevitable and to be expected. We hope you will have success in reducing this to manageable levels and have it work for you rather than against you.

In conclusion remember;

1. You are *not alone*. Many tread this same path and have felt the way you feel when the going gets heavy.
2. There are a variety of good self care strategies in this workbook and in other places which may help lighten your load, but only if you go beyond reading about them and *actually put them into daily practice*.
3. This is an ongoing process and you will need to attend to these issues and work at self-care *intentionally and with energy for the duration of your work life*, but it will be well worth the effort.

Best of luck in your continuing journey and, as an old Irish blessing says, "May the road rise with you."

References

American Association for Marriage and Family Therapy. (2012). Code of Ethics. Retrieved June 2, 2014 from:http://www.aamft.org/imis15/Documents/AAMFT%20Code_11_2012_Secured.pdf

American Counseling Association. (2014). Code of Ethics. Retrieved June 2, 2014 from: http://www.counseling.org/docs/ethics/2014-aca-code-of-ethics.pdf?sfvrsn=4

American Psychological Association. (2010). Ethical principles of psychologists and code of conduct. Retrieved June 2, 2014 from: http://www.apa.org/ethics/code/index.aspx

Bahrer-Kohler, E. (Ed.). (2013). *Burnout for experts: Prevention in the context of living and working*. New York: Springer.

Beck, A.T., Rush, A.J., Shaw, B.F., & Emery, G. (1979). *Cognitive therapy of depression*. New York: Guilford Press.

Beck, A.T., Freeman, A., & Davis, D.D. (2003). *Cognitive therapy for personality disorders*. (2nd ed.). New York: Guilford Press.

Beck, J.S. (2005). *Cognitive therapy with challenging cases: What to do when the basics don't work*. New York: Guilford Press.

Beyond Blue. (2013). National mental health survey of doctors and medical students. www.beyondblue.org

Borritz, M., Rugulies, R., Bjorner, J., Villadsen, M., Mikelson, O.A., & Kristensen, T. (2006). Burnout among employees in human service work; Design and baseline findings. The PUMA study. *Journal of Public Health, 34*, 49-58.

Catherall, D.R. (1995). Coping with secondary traumatic stress: The importance of the therapist's professional peer group. In B.H. Stamm (Ed.), *Secondary traumatic stress: Self-care issues for clinicians, researchers and educators*, (pp. 257-276). Baltimore: Sidran Press.

Chodron, P. (1994). *Start where you are: A guide to compassionate living*. Boston: Shambhala Press, Inc.

Clay, R.A. (2011). Is stress getting to you? *Monitor of the American Psychological Association, 42*, (1) 58-59.

Cooper, C.L., & Williams, S. (1994). (Eds.). *Creating healthy work organizations*. London, U.K.: John Wiley and Sons.

Cushway, D., & Tyler, P. (1994). Stress and coping in clinical psychologists. *Stress Medicine, 10*, 35-40.

Ellis, A. (1983). How to deal with your most difficult client--you. *Journal of Rational Emotive Therapy, 1*, 3-8.

Epstein, R., & Bower, T. (1997, July) Why shrinks have problems. *Psychology Today, 30,*50-60

Evans, S., Huxley, P., Gately, C., et al. (2006). Mental health, burnout and job satisfaction among mental health social workers in England and Wales. *British Journal of Psychiatry, 188,* 75-80.

Farber, B. (Ed.). (1983). *Stress and burnout in human service professionals.* New York: Pergamon Press.

Figley, R. (2002). Compassion fatigue: Psychotherapists' chronic lack of self care. *Journal of Clinical Psychology, 58,* 1433-1441.

Fortener, R.B. (1990). *Relationship between work setting, client prognosis, suicide ideation and burnout in psychologists and counselors.* Unpublished doctoral dissertation, University of Toledo.

Freudenburger, H. (1983). *Burnout: The high cost of high achievement.* Norwell, MA: Anchor Books

Guy, J. (1987). *The personal life of the psychotherapist.* New York: John Wiley and Sons.

Guy, J.D., Poelstra, P.L., & Stark, M.J. (1988). Personal therapy for psychotherapists before and after entering professional practice: A national survey of factors related to its utilization. *Professional Psychology Research and Practice, 19,* 474-476.

Herman, J. (1997). *Trauma and Recovery: The Aftermath of Violence—From Domestic Abuse to Political Terror,* New York. Basic Books.

Hinshaw, S. (Ed.). (2008). *Breaking the silence: Mental health professionals disclose their personal and family experience with mental illness.* New York: Guilford Press.

Kabat-Zinn, J. (2005). *Coming to our senses: Healing ourselves and the world through mindfulness.* New York: Hyperion Books.

Kottler, J. (1999). *The therapist's workbook: Self assessment, self care and self improvement exercises for mental health professionals.* San Francisco: Joey-Bass.

Klareich, E. (1990). *Work without stress.* New York: Bruner-Mazel.

Larson, D.G. (1993). *The helper's journey.* Champaign, IL: Research Press.

Layden, M.A., Newman, C.F., Freeman, A., & Morse, S.B. (1993). *Cognitive therapy of borderline personality disorder.* Boston: Allyn & Bacon.

Leahy, R.L. (2001). *Overcoming resistance in cognitive therapy.* New York: Guilford Press.

Leahy, R.L. (2003). *Roadblocks in cognitive therapy: Transforming challenges into opportunities for change.* New York: Guilford Press.

Lederer, D., & Hall, M. (1990). *Instant relaxation: How to reduce stress at work, at home and in your daily life.* London, U.K.: Crown House.

Leiter, M.P., & Maslach, C. (2005). *Banishing burnout. Six strategies for improving your relationship with work.* San Francisco: Jossey Bass.

Ludgate, J.W. (2012). *Heal yourself: CBT strategies to reduce distress and increase therapeutic effectiveness.* Sarasota, FL: Professional Resources Press.

Maslach, C., Jackson, S.E., & Leiter, M.P. (1996). *The Maslach Burnout Inventory: Manual.* Palo Alto, CA: Consulting Psychologists Press.

Mashlach, C. (1982). *Burnout: The cost of caring.* New York; Prentice Hall.

Maslach, C., & Leiter, M.P. (1997). *The truth about burnout: How organizations cause personal stress and what to do about it.* San Francisico: Jossey-Bass.

Mathieu, F. (2011). *The compassion fatigue workbook: Creative tools for transforming compassion fatigue and vicarious traumatization.* New York: Routledge.

McCann, L., & Pearlman, L.A. (1990). Vicarious traumatization: A framework for understanding the psychological effects of working with victims. *Journal of Traumatic Stress, 3,* 131-149.

Miller, D. (2000). *Dying to care: Work stress and burnout in HIV/AIDS Professionals.* London: Routledge Press.

Miller, W.R. & Rollnick, S. (2002). *Motivational interviewing: Preparing people for Change.* (2nd ed.). New York: Guilford Press.

Moore, K.A., & Cooper, C.L. (1996). Stress in mental health professionals; A theoretical overview. *International Journal of Social Psychiatry, 6(1),* 55-66.

Norcross, J.C., & Guy, J.D. (2007). *Learning to leave it at the office: A guide to psychotherapist self care.* New York: Guilford Press.

Ochberg, F.M. (1991). Post-traumatic therapy. *Psychotherapy: Theory, Research, Practice, Training. 28,* 1, 5-15.

Onyett, S., Pillinger, T., & Muijen, M. (1997). Job satisfaction and burnout among members of community mental health teams. *Journal of Mental Health, 6,* 55-66.

Pearlman, L.A. (1995). Self-care for trauma therapists: Ameliorating vicarious traumatization. In B.H. Stamm (Ed.), *Secondary traumatic stress: Self-care issues for clinicians, researchers and educators* (pp.51-64). Lutherville, MD: Sidran Press.

Pearlman, L.A., & MacIan, P.S. (1995). Vicarious traumatization: An empirical study of the effects of trauma work on trauma therapists. *Professional Psychology Research and Practice, 26,* 558-565.

Prochaska, J.O. & DiClemente, C.C. (1984). *The transtheoretical approach. Crossing traditional boundaries of therapy.* Homewood, IL: Dow Jones- Irwin.

Pines, A., & Maslach, C. (1978). Characteristics of staff burnout in mental health settings. *Hospital and Community Psychiatry, 29,* 233-237.

Pines, A., & Aronson, E. (1988). *Career burnout: Causes and cures.* New York: The Free Press.

Rees, D.W., & Cooper, C.L. (1992). Occupational stress in health service employees. *Health Services Management Research, 3*, 163-172.

Remen, R.N. (2006). *Kitchen table wisdom: Stories that heal.* New York: Riverhead Books

Rippere, V., & Williams, R. (Eds.). (1985). *Wounded healers: Mental health workers' experience of depression.* Chicester: John Wiley and Sons.

Saakvitne, K.W., & Pearlman, L.A. (1996). *Transforming the pain: A workbook on vicarious traumatization.* New York: Norton Professional Books.

Sherbun, M. (2005). *Caring for the caregiver: Eight truths to prolong your career.* Burlington, MA: Jones & Bartlett Learning.

Shinn, M., Rosario, M., March, H., & Chesnutt, D.E. (1984). Coping with job stress and burnout in the human services. *Journal of Personality and Social Psychology, 46*, 864-876.

Skovholt, T.M., & Trotter-Mathison, M. (2011). *The resilient practitioner: Burnout prevention and self-care strategies for counselors, therapists, teachers and health professionals* (2nd ed.). New York: Routledge Press.

Stamm, B.H. (2003). *Secondary traumatic stress: Self-care issues for clinicians, researchers and educators.* Eau Claire, WI: PESI Healthcare.

Wicks, P. (2006). *Overcoming secondary stress in medical and nursing practice: A Guide to professional resilience and personal wellbeing.* New York: Oxford University Press.

Wilson, K.G. (2008). *Mindfulness for two: An acceptance and commitment therapy approach to mindfulness in psychotherapy.* Oakland, CA: New Harbinger Publications.

Wood, B., Klein, S., Cross, H.J., Lammers, C.J., & Elliot, J.K. (1985). Impaired practitioners: Psychologists' perceptions about prevalence and proposals for intervention. *Professional Psychology: Research and Practice, 16*, 843-850.

Yalom, I.D. (2002). *The gift of psychotherapy: An open letter to a new generation of therapists and their patients.* New York: Harper-Collins.

Further Reading

Bahrer-Kohler, E. (Ed.). (2013). *Burnout for experts: Prevention in the context of living and working*. New York: Springer.

Baker, E. (2003). *Caring for ourselves: A therapist's guide to personal and professional well-being*. Washington, DC: American Psychological Association.

Chernis, C. (1995). *Beyond burnout*. New York: Routledge Press.

Kottler, J. (1999). *The therapist's workbook: Self assessment, self care and self improvement exercises for mental health professionals*. San Francisco: Jossey-Bass.

Ludgate, J.W. (2012). *Heal yourself: CBT strategies to reduce distress and increase therapeutic effectiveness*. Sarasota, FL: Professional Resources Press.

Mathieu, F. (2011). *The compassion fatigue workbook: Creative tools for transforming compassion fatigue and vicarious traumatization*. New York: Routledge.

McConnell, E.A. (Ed.). (1982). *Burnout in the nursing profession*. St Louis: Mosby.

Norcross, J.C., & Guy, J.D. (2007). *Learning to leave it at the office: A guide to psychotherapist self care*. New York: Guilford Press.

Rothchild, B. (2006). *Help for the helper. The psychophysiology of compassion fatigue and vicarious trauma*. New York: W.W. Norton & Co.

Sherbun, M. (2005). *Caring for the caregiver: Eight truths to prolong your career*. Burlington, MA: Jones & Bartlett Learning.

Skovholt, T.M., & Trotter-Mathison, M. (2011). *The resilient practitioner: Burnout prevention and self-care strategies for counselors, therapists, teachers and health professionals* (2nd ed.). New York: Routledge Press.

Made in the USA
Middletown, DE
20 November 2017